Steven's

Gift

*A Mother and Son's
Story of Afterlife
Connection*

Denise Willis

BALBOA.
PRESS

A DIVISION OF HAY HOUSE

Balboa Press books may be ordered through booksellers or by contacting:

Balboa Press
A Division of Hay House
1663 Liberty Drive
Bloomington, IN 47403
www.balboapress.com
1 (877) 407-4847

Because of the dynamic nature of the Internet, any web addresses or links contained in this book may have changed since publication and may no longer be valid. The views expressed in this work are solely those of the author and do not necessarily reflect the views of the publisher, and the publisher hereby disclaims any responsibility for them.

The author of this book does not dispense medical advice or prescribe the use of any technique as a form of treatment for physical, emotional, or medical problems without the advice of a physician, either directly or indirectly. The intent of the author is only to offer information of a general nature to help you in your quest for emotional and spiritual well-being. In the event you use any of the information in this book for yourself, which is your constitutional right, the author and the publisher assume no responsibility for your actions.

Print information available on the last page.

ISBN: 978-1-5043-8465-0 (sc)
ISBN: 978-1-5043-8467-4 (hc)
ISBN: 978-1-5043-8466-7 (e)

Library of Congress Control Number: 2017911420

Balboa Press rev. date: 10/17/2017

Contents

For Steven, with Love.

This book is dedicated to all those that have
suffered the loss of someone they love.
May you find peace within this story and seek the light within
yourself to find the way to your true life's purpose.
I wish you an abundance of love, light, and peace within
as you embark upon your own beautiful journey. xo

Prologue

Carry proud my banner
In every game you play
And know that a cure
Is never far away

The undesired ending
To such a noble fight
It seems a fleeting battle
To be lost to the night

My life has served a purpose
Though short it may have been
The answers you are needing
Are not ifs but whens

So celebrate your victories
And worry not what's lost
There's never any progress
Without the pain of cost

This message was shared with me in September of 2004, eleven months after Steven's passing. A co-worker that I had just met the week prior stopped by my desk one day asking if I might be open to receive a message that he *received* for me. He said it was a gift, a channeled message regarding my son. Of course, I was open to receive that! I quite happily replied, "Yes! Thank you so much. This means a lot to me." I felt that this was truly a beautiful gift to receive from someone who had never even met my son, let alone knew anything about me, and yet still felt comfortable enough to share his gift of receiving messages from loved ones that have crossed over. His message touched me deeply then, and it means even more to me today as I've had a lot more time to learn what it all truly means. I am honored to be able to share it with others and equally as blessed simply by having our paths cross in this lifetime. Thank you, Rob, you truly are an earth angel.

Note: The above message talks about Steven's senior year, the football team and the banners made in his honor for the Light the Night walk that took place the following year after he went home to heaven. When I read this message from Rob I could see Steven in his uniform, proudly wearing his jersey with the number 19 shining bright as if it were painted with glitter and tiny diamonds of light. Bright white light on a royal blue jersey (his school colors), we called his team: Steve's Knights "19". Quite fitting as the high school football team is called the *Blue Knights*.

Steven's Senior Year Football Photo - August 2002
This picture was taken a week prior to diagnosis.

Acknowledgements

For you, my beautiful boy, my guardian angel, my soul connection for all eternity, my darling son, Steven Thomas. This book is for you. You and I have written it together along with our many angels and spirit guides. Without you, this book could never have been written. You are my breath, my light, my heart, and my soul. I know we will always be connected in this beautiful light. I will love you forever, through each and every journey we are destined to embark upon together. Thank you for loving me so much in the past, present, and future. I feel your love within me and all around me... Always.

For you, my darling son, Cody Michael, because you are my sweet angel and you were brought here as a gift for your brother and I to adore. Steven says you are his gift to me as he wished for you for almost ten years. I am so proud of who you are and your ever-tender heart. Steven loves you so much. He could not wait for you to be born so he could love you and teach you about the gifts of life. I do so hope that you will cherish the memories of your brother always. Thank you for loving me and for helping me to stay grounded through it all. We have so much to be thankful for, and so much to do while we are here. Be proud of who you are, and always remember to *Stand Tall*.

For you, Mom, because you always asked me when I was going to write this book. Thank you for loving and believing in me through everything. Thank you for supporting me and my dreams along the way. This story is for you too. It is my gift to you, so that you will always remember how much you are loved, and just how much I wish you so much happiness. This is confirmation that dreams really do come true. And yes, Mom... they are real. You already knew that, and for that, I rejoice along with you. I love you Mom.

For you, Kevin, because you were always there for me, loving me, especially through the most painful of moments of which seemed like an eternity to me. I will always love you for that. Our connection is very special and I will always remember what it feels like to have been loved by you. Thank you for being there even when you were not physically there, I still felt your presence with me and that carried me through in ways you may never know. You once told me that when you truly love someone, it never goes away. Well… you were right. We simply move forward in our lives…but our hearts never truly forget. xo

Preface

In 2008, five years upon Steven's passing, I received a book written by Neale Donald Walsch titled, *The Little Soul and the Sun*. It's a children's parable adapted from *Conversations with God*, as a gift, for my son Cody. This gift came with a beautiful message from the sender: "This is for Cody. It will help him through his grief as it tells the story of where it all begins and he will one day understand the meaning of it all." Naturally, I had to read the story myself before giving it to my son as I know how vastly different we all see things, especially when the topic of religion is discussed. Everyone has a different perspective as to what heaven, hell, God or no God means to them. Trust me; at this point along the journey, I was still questioning all of this myself. I fell in love with the story after reading the very first sentence! Its lightness drew me in and I found that a certain aspect of it truly touched my spirit. It felt like the floodgates of light had opened for me to see my path just a little more clearly. This is the part of the story that helped me to remember what I came here for:

> "I know what I want to be, I know what I want to be!" the Little Soul announced with great excitement. "I want to be the part of special called 'forgiving.' I want to experience myself as that." "Good." Said God, "But there's one thing you should know." The Little Soul was becoming a bit impatient now. It always seemed as though there were some complication. "What is it?" the Little Soul sighed. "There is no one to forgive." "No one?" the Little Soul could hardly believe what had been said. "No one!" God repeated. "Everything I have made is perfect. There is not a single soul in all creation less perfect than you. Look

around you." It was then that the Little Soul realized a large crowd had gathered. Souls had come from far and wide – from all over the Kingdom – for the word had gone forth that the Little Soul was having this extraordinary conversation with God, and everyone wanted to hear what they were saying. Looking at the countless other souls gathered there, the Little Soul had to agree. None appeared less wonderful, less magnificent, or less prefect than the Little Soul itself. Such was the wonder of the souls gathered around and so bright was their Light, that the Little Soul could scarcely gaze upon them. "Who, then, to forgive?" asked God. "Boy this is going to be no fun at all!" grumbled the Little Soul. "I wanted to know what that part of special felt like." And the Little Soul learned what it must feel like to be sad. But just then, a Friendly Soul stepped forward from the crowd. "Not to worry, Little Soul," the Friendly Soul said, "I will help you." "Why, I can give you something to forgive." "You can?" "Certainly!" chirped the Friendly Soul. "I can come into your next lifetime and do something for you to forgive." "But why? Why would you do that?" the Little Soul asked. "You, who are a Being of such utter perfection! You, who vibrate with such a speed that it creates a Light so bright that I, can hardly gaze upon you! What could cause you to want to slow down your vibration to such a speed that your bright Light would become dark and dense? What could cause you – who are so light that you dance upon the stars and move throughout the Kingdom with the speed of your thought – to come into my life and make yourself so heavy that you could do this bad thing?" "Simple," the Friendly Soul said. "I would do it because I love you." The Little Soul seemed surprised at the answer. "Don't be so amazed," said the Friendly Soul, "you have done the same thing for me. Don't you remember? Oh, we have danced together, you and I, many times. Through the eons and across all the ages have we danced. Across all time and in many places, have we played together. You just don't remember. We have both been All Of It. We have been the Up and the Down of it, the Left and the Right of it. We have been the Here and the Thereof it, the Now and Then of it. We have been the male and the female, the good and the bad – we have both been the victim and the villain of it. Thus, we have come together, you and I, many times before; each bringing to the other the exact and perfect opportunity to Express and to Experience Who We Really Are. "And so," the Friendly Soul explained a little further, "I will come into your next lifetime and be the 'bad one' this time. I will do something really terrible, and then you can experience yourself as the One Who Forgives." "But what will you do? the Little Soul asked, just a little nervously, that will be so terrible?" "Oh," replied the Friendly Soul with a twinkle, "we'll think of something." Then the Friendly Soul seemed to turn serious, and said in a quiet voice, "You are right about one thing, you know." "What is that?" the Little Soul wanted to know. "I will have to slow down my vibration and become very heavy to do this not-so-nice thing. I will have to pretend to be something very unlike myself. And so, I have but one favor to ask of you in return." "Oh, anything, anything!" cried the Little Soul, and began to dance and sing, "I get to be forgiving, I get to be forgiving!" Then the Little Soul saw that the Friendly Soul was remaining very quiet. "What is it?" the Little Soul asked. "What can I do for you? You are such an angel to be willing to do this for me!" "Of course, this Friendly Soul is an angel!" God interrupted. "Everyone is! Always remember: I have sent you nothing but angels."

As soon as I finished reading this beautifully illustrated book, something amazing happened. In my mind, or more so, what appeared to be a very vivid dream, only in the light of day, I saw an image of Steven and me in heaven, or, at least, what I dreamt heaven might look like if it were, in fact, a real place. In any case, I am looking forward to seeing this place for myself one day and will certainly be making note to visit this place within heaven in which Steven and I shared this conversation:

"Okay Mom, please try and remember that when you are born, you won't know me until I am born to you while you are quite young. You will know the special connection we share as you will not have this with any of your other children. When it's time for me to come home to heaven again, you won't remember this conversation, so my illness will consume your very beautiful heart and soul. The grief will be debilitating and you will have to learn how to connect to me and to spirit once again. It will be hard, and I will help you. Please try and not get too involved with the earthly world so that you forget about the angels, the guides, God, and me. Once you remember why I chose to be born and why you chose to have me, you will remember our gift and you will share it with the world because it needs light workers and earth angels Mom, and you have to show the grieving families and others connected to them, how to survive and move forward along their life's journey. You can help them to learn how to heal and to make their lives better so that they too can help others and live the lives they were meant to with peace in their hearts. You can use your gifts on levels much bigger than most can comprehend. Please Mom, don't forget. I will always be with you, helping you and helping the children. Together we can make a difference and help to make the world a better place. I love you Mom… Always."

This conversation took place with Steven and me sitting side by side on a magnificent rock surrounded by the most beautiful ocean filled with soft, beautiful, turquoise-blue water. There were so many teeny-tiny pearly shells that all seemed to glisten like diamonds so eloquently placed upon the sand. They were everywhere; as if they were each specifically hand-placed by the angels themselves. I could smell the sweet, salty essence of the sparkling water as it permeated the air. The colors in the sky were such a beautiful pale blue with clouds of soft pink and lavender. I have never seen such vibrant colors such as these. They made an imprint within my mind that I will always cherish. I have often wished I could paint simply so that I could capture my dreams and turn them into reality to surround myself with and bask in their beauty as a daily reminder of what life truly is all about. A rare beauty to never be forgotten. This dream will forever be etched into my heart and soul as this truly is where our story begins.

Introduction

This is *our* story. It tells of a time in which I felt my life was over upon the death of my son. My journey from that point until the present moment has been quite a rough and extremely bumpy road. I found little solace out there when searching for the words that would help me to get through my grief and despair. I literally read everything I could get my hands on and still nothing really helped me. I felt like I was opening every door along this path in my life just hoping that something would appear along the way that might suggest some sense of peace and solace. I began keeping a journal, writing down my dreams, my thoughts and all the many mixed emotions I experienced during the first year upon Steven's death on October 11, 2003. Eventually, the journal morphed itself into this story. My story... His story... Our story... and ultimately, it then became *Steven's Gift*.

The path is clearly written along the way in this story and does expose some very tough moments. One will absolutely be able to see the growth to healing. It's not a *heavy* read for there were some incredibly beautiful moments that took place along the way as well. It is my life's purpose and my mission to help people so that they can learn to help themselves along their path of healing and connecting to their spirit within. Even if you have never lost a child, or anyone else for that matter, this story can still help to assist with guiding you to seek deeper within yourself to learn about who you are and what you are truly here for. Please remember this most important fact; healing comes from within and only you can make that happen by taking the first step in being open, ready, and willing to receive abundant love and light and to also release all that no longer serves you for yourself and for your highest good. You have to take the first step on your own. Grief can consume us if we let it. It is my deepest wish, and hope, that simply by reading this story, you may find that we are not so different from one another and that just maybe my experience will help you to seek your own truth. You are not alone. You never were and you will never, ever, feel that way again. There are so many others out there just like you and me, and it's time that we all connect deeper within ourselves and support each other along the way. Because after all, life is a journey and we are all connected in some way. So why not support one another along the way with love in our hearts. To me, there is no greater gift.

Before I begin with the *nitty gritty*, I want to share a little of my own life's history with you. I'll start at the beginning so that you'll get a better picture of who I am and why I chose this path in life in which I am walking upon today. But first, I'll begin with my Steven.

Steven Thomas

Simply writing his name brings a warm smile to my face. What a beautiful soul. He came into my life when I was just eighteen. How ironic that he would then leave me at the tender age of eighteen himself. Eighteen... Wow! How sad it is for me to write this and speak these words aloud. I buried my beautiful son before he even had the chance to graduate high school. Of course, I know how blessed I am to have had him in my life for those glorious eighteen years, and yet I still feel so much of the pain and deep despair of tragedy having had to let him go before I was ready to say good-bye. But what mother is ever actually truly ready to say good-bye to their child? No matter what their age is or in which path they took in leaving us, having to say good-bye to one of our own children is a horrific feeling that crushes the heart into a billion pieces. It is an emotion that is physically felt and no one else can truly understand, let alone comprehend this kind of pain unless they have experienced it for themselves.

I have always known that Steven was, and still is, a very special soul, an earth angel, if you will. I felt this way since the very beginning, from the moment of conception. The moment the sperm met the egg, my entire body trembled with a warm and overall tingly vibrational sensation. I remember saying to his father, "Wow... did you feel that?" I loved that he felt it too. This feeling stayed with me and I knew I was already carrying a very special angel. Can you imagine what an amazingly beautiful feeling that is? Going through pregnancy and waiting anxiously for every single movement to occur within me simply so I could feel even more connected to my baby. I was due on December 22, 1984. That day came and went, and just when I thought I absolutely could not wait another day, my little angel arrived, and I just could not believe my eyes. Steven Thomas was born after twenty-two hours of labor, on January 5, 1985. It was a very cold blizzard-like winter's day. This much waited for, sweet angel baby, finally arrived with his soft, peachy skin and rose kissed cheeks. He had tiny little dimples framing his beautiful soft pink lips. He was all aglow for me to just completely fall in love with. The tears came quickly, so intensely, carrying with them the most glorious feelings of warmth, joy, compassion, and such a powerfully strong feeling of abundant love. Complete and utterly glorious unconditional love. This is an emotion and connection that truly cannot be experienced by anyone other than that of a mother.

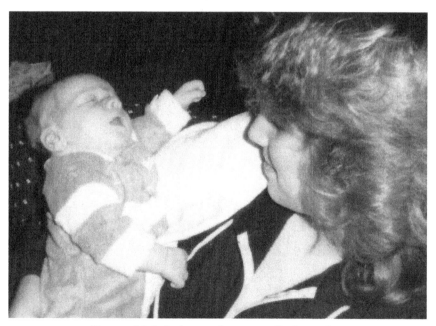

You and Me kid, together we will always be.

Not to worry, this story is not going to be about a mother glorifying her dead son's life and turning it into a *super hero* novel. It's not even about me trying to explain my interpretation of why I think our children have to die or why I think they are all still here with us. It's not about sharing yet another tragic life lost to cancer, nor running a massive crusade in trying to find a cure for it either. It is not about *finding God* or making peace with death. It's not even about trying to heal from my deep seeded feelings of abundant anger, sadness, guilt, and pain, although I certainly went through all those emotions and so very many more. This is a story about love, life, death, and the afterlife connection and what I have personally learned and experienced throughout the process of living my *new* life today. My *new* path. My *infinite journey* here on earth. I wanted to share my story, Steven's story, so that others out there whom have suffered the loss of a child may also find hope and know that their life is a journey, and that their journey is connected to their loved ones that have crossed over just as my son did. Such a connection is quite real; this I can attest to. You too can experience this connection. It's time for you to find this peace within. This is where it all begins anyway, deep within you, within your spirit, the very heart and soul of who you are.

This story is about *Steven's Gift*. The gift he gave me upon his death. His life had meaning, his death had purpose, and his mission here on earth was one of greatness. He had a plan, and he also had a plan for me as well.

Chapter 1

The Beginning

Saturday, April 1, 2006

After three years of journaling since Steven's death, today is the first day I am finally able to sit down and write this story, *our story*. This is a story I have recited at least a million times within my own mind. Each and every time I try to compose my thoughts, set up my laptop in just the right place, pour myself a cup of tea, and start to type the words I've so longed to share, I am troubled by my ever-aching heart. My eyes well up with tears that I continue to fight off every waking moment since the day that I lost him. I begin my story every time, with the same questions sent directly to him:

> "My beautiful boy, my little, blond, blue-eyed, angel, how I wish I could find a way to handle the pain, to heal my heart, and somehow try to find a way to mend that deep black hole that took over my heart when you left this place to go where you are in eternal peace. You see, I do know that you are happy there. I also know that I had to let you go before you could say good-bye. I did not want to. I wanted to pretend that you were still in the hospital and would eventually open your eyes and say, 'Hi Mom, can we go home now?' But that day never came. I had to stand by your bedside and watch the color drain from

your beautiful face. A face I knew so well. One that I've looked at and adored for eighteen years and ten months. You had my cheeks. You had my smile. You even shared my love for the little things in life. You had the most amazingly beautiful blue eyes. Eyes that mirrored every single emotion in which you felt, even when you wanted to hide behind them. I always knew what you were thinking and feeling as if we were connected, "twin-like". I often wondered if you felt that too.

Did you know that when you left me, a huge part of my soul left with you? The only way to describe the emptiness I feel is to picture a heart full of love and life and fullness surrounded by beautiful light and utter joy and then to take that heart and rip it brutally from deep within me, leaving a huge, gaping, black hole of despair. All that love left me when you did. Where did you go? Do you have my heart there with you? Why did you have to leave me taking that piece of my heart that does not allow me to see you, where I cannot hear your voice or feel your heart beat when I hold you close? Are you holding it with you now, until we can be together wherever you are? You see, honey, there is a magnificent and beautiful feeling of love, contentment, peace, and a strong sense of knowing one will never be alone when having a child. One holds that joy deep within when becoming a mother. I felt that when I was pregnant with you. I was so young, and yet every single moment that you were growing inside me, I came to know you for who you are… an angel. My angel.

As hard as it is for me to sit here, writing this and trying not to cry, I know it has to be done. I know you have been waiting a long time for this moment to come, the time when I could write from my heart, along with your help as well, of course, but to finally find a place in my life where my strength would keep me from crumbling into a million tiny pieces. Today is that day, my sweetheart. I love you more than anything in the world. I miss you so very much, and will continue to every single moment of my life. I know when you are near me, and I know when you are guiding me along my path in life. I promise I will try to be quiet enough to hear you and to listen to what it is that you need for me to know."

I've had so many people try to offer me advice on how to grieve, telling me how my son is in a better place and is not sick anymore. That he is always with me, that he is doing God's work now and that only the "special" die young. Blah, blah, blah... all the pep talks...the many conversations, therapy sessions, the hiding out in your room, lying on your bed just to breathe in the scent of you on your pillow. The running away, and everything else that I've tried, have not helped me to heal this hole in my heart. Every single book I have been given, not to mention all the ones I purchased on how to handle grief seem so insignificant to me, like there is no depth, as if people are trying to tell me to just believe in God and everything will be okay, and that all I need is time, and to just have faith. Don't they know how hollow that all sounds? Unless they have walked in these "death of a child" shoes of mine, trust me, they have no damn clue of what I am feeling.

Most have no idea of the gifts that I hold deep within my soul, the "knowing" that I have carried with me throughout my entire life. The truth in what we know about that exists after death. I wanted to tell them all to shut the hell up, to just be quiet and let me breathe, let me think, let me go through my emotions all by myself. It's not easy for me to push forward, but it gives me strength to know what has to be done and knowing where my son is now. You see, the gift I have is also within my Steven. It is also within my son Cody. Being intuitive, having the gift of knowing, seeing, and feeling the other side. These are the gifts/blessings that we three share together.

I know Steven is standing beside me right now as I am writing this. I can feel him. So, I asked him, "Do you remember the day that you were standing with your hand on the door handle to your room downstairs? It was a Saturday in the fall of September 2003. I was getting ready to take your brother to his baseball game. You asked me where I was going and it was at that exact moment that I knew you wanted me to stay home."

Steven responded, "Yes Mom, I remember. And yes, you are right, we are always connected." I knew that when we looked into each other's eyes we were connected and reading each other's thoughts and emotions at that very moment. I thought, "Oh my God, this is it. This is the last weekend we will stand here face to face and be able to have a conversation like this." I was so scared. I felt paralyzed, terrified, and unable to breathe. It seemed like forever before we broke that connection. He went back to his room, and I left the house to go to Cody's game. I kept my cell phone in my pocket the whole time, checking it every two minutes. I knew Steven would be calling shortly after I left the house, and when he did, the first question he asked me was when we would be home because he wanted to hang out with his "little guy". He said that it had been a while since he had done that. He was so sweet. My heart was breaking because I knew it was the calm before the storm.

I heard him talking to Cody while they were building Bionicles together at the kitchen table. He said, "Don't worry buddy, Mom will always be here with you. Mom will always take care of you just like she did me. She'll always be there, no matter what. Don't worry about your dad. I know how you feel because he and I used to be pretty close, too. He was a pretty cool guy, and we had a lot of fun together. But right now, he just needs this time for himself." When Cody asked about him being there for him Steven paused before telling him that he would always be with him. It broke my heart to hear him speak with so much love in his voice, telling his brother that he would always be with him. I think we all knew this was the end of his time here with us. Even though Cody was so young back then (age eight), he never forgot what his big brother said to him on that day. I thank you Steven, I thank you for reminding your brother how much you and I love him and always will.

My story, thus far, must be bringing out the fear that so many of you may carry within your own heart. You may even be thinking, *I cannot imagine what I would do if it was my child*, or, *thank God, it's not me*. Tell me, can you truly ever even begin to imagine what that kind of pain feels like without having gone through it yourself? Or, just maybe; you are reading this because you do know what it feels like having lost a child of your own. If that's the case, then please know that my heart goes out to you. I sincerely hope that my story helps you to find that peace within yourself so that you can continue to grow upon your life's journey with love, peace, and happiness, just as I have. I am also sending you a huge hug right now. You will always have a friend in me should you ever want to reach out and talk. I would love to support all those that I can. To me, this is one of life's greatest gifts. To be able to offer others some sense of support along their journeys to help them find a way to live their best lives. This is my life's journey.

I have read many books. I've searched the internet for days on end, hoping to find that one special bereavement group. I searched for the best doctor, psychotherapist, PhD, psychic, life coach, the very best meditation music, the most well-known, and successful spiritual mediums. I even searched for the right circle of people, hoping they could help me find some sense of peace within myself. All of which gave me little solace other than to teach me that I had to learn to really dig deep within myself, before I could even begin to try to figure it all out. I had no idea how much I had to heal within my own soul, my spirit within.

This story is told from everything that I know and believe to be true. To be real and honest as it comes from deep within my heart. It's meant to be shared, with the hope, that someone else out there who has also shared the loss of a child, can find peace and comfort in knowing that they are not alone, and that their beloved child, no matter what the age, or reason, for their passing, is in a beautiful place. It's a story that I hope will touch many lives, parents, siblings, dear friends, and anyone else who has a heart. More importantly, to know that our loved ones are here with us, simply because, they never truly left us in the first place.

Love stays deep within our soul even when we leave our earthly form. I can say this to you not simply as just a belief, but as a truth. A truth that I have discovered, through my own son's passing. I wonder how many other parents out there who have lost their children also knew many years before their death that they would not get to see their child graduate from high school, or be able to see them get married, and have a family of their own. Maybe that is something that can only be seen through the eyes of an intuitive person. But then again, maybe not. It would still be nice to get to talk to those who have shared this experience. Some stories are so guarded, so edited, so small in significance, so jaded, and fairy-tale like. I want to talk to those with the real story, the un-edited version. The real truth.

How can a true-life story be so deeply changed with editing? Except for some grammatical and punctuation corrections, and maybe even some spelling mishaps, how can someone who has no idea what all this is about, or what it feels like, simply edit a story written from the depth of one's heart and soul? Is it to sell more books by cleaning up the verbiage so it reads with most perfect little etiquette style and equally as perfect content? To pique the interest of those who need to read a story with more tears and pain? Is that what sells? Are people more interested in sex, drugs, violence, and politics? I think we may have missed the boat at times in that sense. We are all human beings. We all have a heart, a soul, a body, a mind, and a life. We are all here on earth to live out our life's purpose, our journey, no matter what it may be. A life should count for something after we're gone, so why not have it count while we are still here.

It should not take the death of a child or someone else we love to guide us onto a new enlightened path. Why can't we live each day to the fullest and not be so caught up in the rat race that we just hurry through each day never knowing why we are here in the first place. You know, I never truly realized how self-absorbed people can be. How lost so many are, living in just their egos without even realizing it, or what's worse, not even caring to even consider that there may be more to living than just the way they are living today. Living out each workweek just to get to the weekend so they can finally have some time to do what they really love. Is that what life is truly all about? I'm shocked by how quickly people forget the things that matter most in life. The ways in which they shut out the things that they don't want to listen to or to even try to see with some sense of depth.

It's time to dig deep. It's time to listen to your heart, and truly hear all that it has to say. Don't wait. Start today. It's never too late to move forward and begin a new journey. Are you living the life you always dreamed of? If you aren't, why not? You can make your life be anything you want it to be. You just have to want it and to make it happen within your heart and soul first. Have faith in yourself. Start by making your wish list. Don't leave anything out. Let the words flow from your heart... the rest will follow quite easily.

I know that I gave birth to Steven to share a life with him. To learn from one another, and to share a beautiful bond as most families do. The beginning of a life is always the best of times it seems, and yet we know we are all born for a purpose. It's just not easy to remember what that is sometimes. I only wish we knew this before tragedy came to remind me in a much more difficult way. It is a learning process, living this life, which is for damn sure. If we could all learn to connect deeper within ourselves right from the start, then maybe, just maybe, the pain of loss would be a little less, if not completely accepted, and understood.

Chapter 2

The Angel Within

I can remember almost every detail of my life since I was a child. The way the kitchen smelled when my mother was cooking dinner, the images of the kitchen walls covered in wallpaper, encompassed in a bright 1970's yellow and orange fruit pattern. I can even remember the soft blue bathroom tiles and the way all three of my siblings and I fought for our time in that bathroom getting ready for school, or simply to just have some alone time. For me, my favorite alone time, was spent lounging in the bathtub. I filled it to the rim, with strawberry scented bubbles that were always just daring to grow and trickle over the side of the tub.

That was a glorious time. Spending hours in the bubbles, engrossed in a *Nancy Drew* or *Hardy Boys* story, continuously emptying the water as it got cold, and adding more hot water at the same time, of course, using my feet to turn the knobs as I refused to look up from my book nor be interrupted by using my hands to turn the knobs. This was my freedom from everything in the real world. My magical journey travelling through a storybook filled with so much hope and adventure that always transformed me to another place in time within my own imagination. I loved the way reading completely took me away from my own world so completely that it allowed me to escape my life even if for only a little while.

To me, this is one of the best ways to escape reality. I used to dream of being in a big, beautiful, castle library, lounging by the fire, reading all day and all night. Just my imagination and me, time travelling through so many stories, travelling all over the world.

Me and my favorite book on Christmas day. I was 2 ½ years old.

Many of my childhood memories are painful ones filled with my parent's own life's drama inflicted upon us children, and some memories are of a very normal and happy time spent with my friends, cousins, and grandparents. Some of my favorite memories are the ones that are encompassed by my time spent with my sweet Grammy Lois. I am pretty sure that I adored her from the moment I came into this world. I have always felt so connected to her and her beautiful spirit. Most days, I never felt as if I belonged, or fit in when I was at home with my mom and siblings. I always felt out of my element, out of my comfort zone, and so very much out of place. I do not truly remember ever really feeling like our home was a fun and happy place to be. I remember feeling like I was always walking on eggshells around my mom as she always seemed so unhappy. I never wanted to do anything to make her upset with me. I remember wishing there was more that I could do to make her happy. It was hard to just be myself, but then again, maybe we just didn't know how to communicate what we were feeling deep inside back then.

I spent as much time as I could dreaming, wishing, reading, and praying to turn eighteen as quickly as I could so I could move out and start my life, have a family of my own, to love, and feel that love in return. Sure, friends and family were around, most were just living their own lives since children were most often seen but rarely heard in my family. I often wondered why there were four of us when there was such sadness in my mother's heart. Were we there to make her life better, or were we there just because three girls came first and then finally, the long-awaited son that was supposed to make the picture complete and perfect arrived? I often wonder why people choose to give birth to a child. What goes through a woman's mind when she creates a life? Does she really think that having a child will make her life better? Does every woman feel in her heart that she is fulfilling her life's purpose by pro-creating? Is it a path that was chosen for her long before she was born? I often wonder if my mother has this all figured out yet.

It seems so simple to me at this point in my own life. I often think of what life would have been like for me had I gone back in time and changed even one small thing. I am very thankful for my life and even more thankful that I had the sense to figure out that it is much too short a time to be here and that living each moment to the fullest is what makes my heart soar and continue onward. There is absolutely nothing that cannot be rendered. Nothing can be so bad that it cannot be overcome. Or at the very least, endured. Some things are much too painful to ever forget, but to learn to make peace with them is the key to releasing much of the painful memories. It took me years to figure that out.

Thinking back to my childhood, nothing stands out in my mind of the very moment in which I knew that I had a gift of knowing, a feeling, an intuition, clairvoyance, and psychic ability. Call it what you will, all are much the same to me. It seems to have always been there, always part of me. Having this gift of knowing, feeling that an event was about to take place in a future yet unseen, was a little unnerving to me. Is this truly a gift that most would consider as such? I do know that my mother also has this gift, and I also know that this has been passed on to her through many generations within our family, for both male, and female. Although I do consider being intuitive a beautiful gift from above, I am not so sure that my mom felt quite the same way. I can remember looking into her eyes and being able to feel her emotions, her sadness, and her pain. I used to feel those emotions so deeply that I thought they were being projected towards me, as if I was also living her pain. It took me many years to figure out that by feeling other's thoughts and emotions was simply just that. A feeling, and simply by feeling these emotions around me, I soon learned that these emotions really had nothing to do with me at all. It can be difficult when you are a child to decipher such emotions especially when there is no one to talk to about it with only makes it harder to accept and to fully understand.

Some days I did have dreams/visions that came true, a time travel of sorts, to places in time that would become a reality for me later on. This was extremely difficult to envision and make sense of. One memory comes to my mind quite vividly. I was travelling with a group of co-workers to an event in Boston. I was the event photographer so I knew that I had to be focused and ready for anything. Before we left the office that day, I remember thinking about my grandfather who was in the hospital very ill with colon cancer. This was just not a good time for my family as he was the patriarch of our family and was quite loved by us all. I stood there in my office gathering my equipment, all the while feeling him with me, and seeing his smile within my mind. As much as that feeling was filled with complete and utter warmth and love, I had the saddest feeling in my heart. I pushed it away and went on with my trip as I knew I had to be there as they were counting on me. I chose to be the driver of a very large school van. Considering its size, and the people on board, I would have to put all my attention into keeping this monstrosity of a vehicle on the road. Everyone was laughing, and talking. Everyone seemed so excited to get to the event and share conversations with the attendees. My friend Elizabeth rode up front to keep me company. We listened to music and laughed while sharing stories.

At 3:24pm, I felt my grandfather near me. He came to say good-bye, and I knew at that moment, that he was gone. I felt it like I was standing there at his bedside with the rest of my family, only I wasn't suffering their grief as I knew he was with me letting me know that he had crossed over. I only felt love and peace surround me. There was no sense of pain, or despair. I later learned that he did actually pass away at that time. Elizabeth noticed my change in mood and focus and she asked, "What's wrong, all the color has drained from your face, are you okay?" I told her my grandfather had just died. She wanted me to pull over and find a phone to call my family. I told her that I would call home when I could speak to them after the event. I needed to stay focused and muster all the grace and professionalism that I could to get through the night. I was so afraid that I would not be able to do it if I spoke with my family before we even got there.

The event was a great success. I circulated everywhere, capturing each moment on film, which was later used in the school's alumni magazine. It was wonderful to see so many people there in support of the school, sharing in the fundraising events, to help support women's education. I always felt so honored to take part in these events. And yet this one felt so completely different. There was such lightness in the air that night. It seemed as if everyone felt it. When it was over, I quickly found a phone and called my aunt's house. My cousin Sara was crying when she answered the phone telling me that Papa had died. When I asked her when, she said, "3:24pm." It was the exact same time that I felt him with me. As much as this seems like a coincidence to so many people, I know better than to diminish it by brushing it off as something so insignificant in that way. I believe that there are no coincidences as these are merely just events and connections that are meant to take place in this way for reasons we are yet to fully understand. Think about it. Why was I able to feel my grandfather's presence at exactly 3:24pm in route to Boston? Why would anyone even think to confirm such a time frame anyway? I feel so blessed to have this type of connection. A little unnerved nonetheless, but still equally as blessed. This certainly is just one of the many experiences I have had over the years.

Another memory, although difficult to envision, was when I was looking at Steven when he was a baby. I just couldn't see him as an adult. I could see him as a young man, but any time I tried to see him as a man, married, with children of his own, I felt nothing but fear, panic, and sadness. I took that as a sign that I was not meant to know the future when it came to him. He was so beautiful, inside and out. I will never, ever, forget feeling such a deep connection and abundance of love for him that began even before he was born. Although I was only eighteen years old, I was not that young in life experience. I had always felt that I was an old soul. I knew in my heart that Steven was going to be very special. I never felt that he would be just a normal little boy. He had an angelic presence right from the start. I chose the name *Steven Thomas* before he was born. I knew that he was going to be a boy, and that he would have blond hair and the most exquisite blue eyes. So, expressive those eyes would become as he grew in age and in wisdom. Eyes I will never forget as long as I live.

My pregnancy was a breeze. My first ultrasound just absolutely elated me. Being able to see my son and every tiny little detail of him moving around within me was such a gift. Those tiny little movements, like little butterfly wings fluttering all around within me, made my heart over flow with happiness and love. The bigger my stomach grew, the stronger the movements became. What a glorious feeling it is to feel your baby's first tiny little movements. Steven was quite an active little one indeed. During the last trimester, I thought for sure that this future football player was going to let himself out sooner than later. But, that didn't happen. Instead of him arriving anywhere even close to his due date, he decided to just simply hang out a little longer. My labor was over twenty-two hours long before he finally arrived by cesarean section. I could not wait to see his sweet little face. I was so excited and yet so exhausted at the same time. And then, there he was. This little light of love appeared right before me. He was so beautiful. He had sweet little peachy cheeks with tiny rosy centers, a little button nose, and soft, tiny, pink lips. His hair was such a golden blond that it looked like an angel's halo. He was magnificent and he melted my heart completely. There is such a special connection that only a mother can feel when her child is born, a special soul connection, and the only words that can describe such emotions are as such: Pure, Abundant, Love.

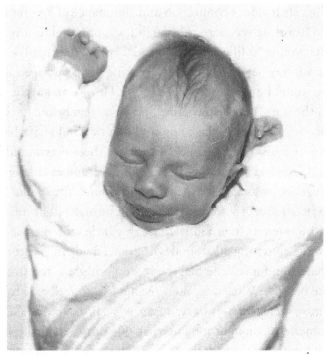

Beautiful You… Steven Thomas. January 5th, 1985

Steven was so alive, so alert, looking around as if to take everything in. When I first saw his face, he looked right into my eyes and I immediately felt his soul coincide with mine and from that moment on, we were connected. We were one. My heart opened like a floodgate full of love and happiness. Such a deep love, it made my heart fill to the brim and beat so strongly within me. If I could have drawn a picture of what my heart looked like at that moment, one would clearly see the beauty within, and all around it. What a glorious image this would be had it been captured on film. This love stays within a mother forever. The connection between a mother and child is one that no one can ever come between nor ever erase; it's a deeply spiritual tie that is bound forever, and ever after.

It's amazing how fast time went by from that day forward. My Grammy Lois came to visit with us and she held Steven the entire time she visited each and every one of the five days that we were in the hospital. She would enter our room with a great big, beautiful smile, full of happiness and so very much love. I just adored her and the way she always made me feel so loved. Steven and I were loved. She was equally as loved too. She brought me a children's bible one day as well as her own because she wanted to show me the meaning of Steven's name. That meant so much to me. To have her there and to see her face shine with such love while she held my little angel. Steven, Crowned one. What a fitting name to describe him and his essence. The nurses just loved this sweet little boy who was always looking all around him, taking in every single second of his new life. There was one nurse that came to see us every day. She called him Little Stevie. She held him when I had visitors because back then, babies could not be in the room while visitors were there. I didn't like that at all. I just wanted everyone to go away so that I could hold him all the time. They always made an exception when Grammy Lois visited during the day. She said it was her gift.

Steven's nurse loved to hold him and tell me all about how sweet he was while he was with them in the nursery. She said that he was very special and that he was her favorite. I wonder if she knew that he was an angel sent from heaven just as I did, and just as all the other babies were as well. I often wonder if she had any idea as to what his journey in this life would be and why he had to come here and carry forth his mission. It's thoughts like this that make me wish I knew then what I know now. I would have asked his nurse more questions. Maybe she had an insight much deeper than I did at that time. I am sure she has seen so much in her many years in the nursery. I would have spent more time talking with her. Maybe she would have shared her stories with me, but then again, I know that everything happens for a reason and each event equally also has its own purpose. Those five days in the hospital were just that, a short time in which to make memories and to open a door to a new path in this life.

Chapter 3

Daily Life

I don't think I ever really spent much time thinking about Steven's future, or what life might have been for him when he was all grown up as I had often felt that we just simply lived in the moment, looking forward to each day, as it brought much fun, and adventure, in all that we did together. I watched my son grow and become this amazing little person who was so happy, all the time. That smile, and those dimples of his were contagious. He was always smiling, and laughing, and often appeared as if he were trying to take in every moment, as if recording it into his memory bank for all eternity. He slept only enough to revive himself before stepping out into the world the next day. He started walking at fifteen months old and I did not worry that this was late in the stages of development as he was perfectly content crawling to any place he so chose. He never felt the need to hurry with anything. He simply took each moment in as it came. I admired that in him. Early each morning I'd go in to his room to see if he was awake. I'd quietly walk through the door and as soon as he could see me, he'd look at up at me, with that beautiful smile of his, blue eyes sparkling like little blue diamonds, and my heart would melt, as I scooped him up from his crib, smothering him with kisses. He always laughed when I kissed his neck. I just adored him. He was adorable. What a joy it was to be with him every day. He was so happy to be playing in his room all by himself, enjoying his toys as if they were all made of magic. Everything elated him and he took time to play with everything he had in his toy chest.

He especially loved to ride his motorcycle all around the house, beeping the horn and laughing. He adored the swing, playing in the sandbox, and spending time with other children, no matter what their age was. I took great delight in seeing his face light up when he had someone to play with. Naturally, he was very nurturing to those who were younger than he was; as if he felt he was supposed to help guide them in some way. This beautiful trait stayed with him throughout his life.

I remember there was one day in which we were playing outside and there was a sweet baby squirrel watching us. It did not scurry away once it knew that we were paying attention to it. It stayed quite close to us. Gently, I called to it, asking it to come see us. And it did. It was adorable, just sitting there watching us without any worry whatsoever. Steven was so delighted; he wanted to hold it so desperately. Suddenly, the squirrel staring coming closer towards us and I immediately heard my mother's voice in my head, "they are not cute, they are rats with bushy tails that carry rabies." I got a little nervous not knowing for sure if it was safe to stay there so close to the little squirrel. I picked Steven up from his playpen, and brought him into the house. I felt so badly having run away from the sweet little squirrel. It must have felt awful watching us leave so abruptly. Steven's heart was broken. I told him that squirrels sometimes were not healthy and that if they got too close, they could easily be frightened and bite us to protect themselves and that could really hurt us. He hugged me tightly. It made me so happy to know how sweet, and sensitive he was. He adored animals as much as I did. They were always part of our lives. If I could go back in time, I would not have listened to that voice in my head, and would have trusted my instincts better and simply just let nature take its course. We never did see the little squirrel again after that day.

A very happy little Steven. This was taken the same
day prior to our meeting the baby squirrel.

Our life was pretty normal for the most part. We had ups and downs just like everyone else did. To me, life simply would just not be normal if people didn't each have their own struggles and triumphs. Steven was not a huge fan of school but he did love sports and seeing his friends. He absolutely hated to read and write. This never made sense to me as every night he would choose a book for me to read to him. He even made me act out the different voices for all the characters in the story. He was very healthy except for the typical childhood minor ailments, a few ear infections and the occasional strep throat. Steven loved playing all types of sports. He played at school and for the town leagues, often wearing the number twelve as he said it was for my birthday. He played baseball, soccer, hockey, basketball, and football. He was part of the ski club and he loved snowboarding, motorcycle riding, bike riding, skateboarding, camping, hiking, wake boarding, tubing, jet skiing, and basically anything and everything that allowed him to have fun and be outside. He loved the water and would often take very long baths just lying in the water, and playing with his cars. These types of activities came so easily to him. You name it, he played it, as he was always down for anything fun. Of course, like anyone else, he loved hanging out watching TV and movies as well as playing video games. He was quite well rounded, that's for sure.

I am very thankful to have been blessed in having such great memory. I can remember moments from such a young age. It's in these memories that I find the ultimate moments of peace and solace. They remind me of the many moments that were so full of love, joy, and happiness. Although many memories are also difficult to think about, I am still thankful that I have them all so beautifully tucked away within the treasure chest of my mind. I know that every memory is there for me to revisit as often as I so choose. Being a parent encompasses so much joy that we tend to take for granted just how quickly our lives are moving forward. Sometimes we tend to live for and through our children, after all, they are our responsibility to raise, nurture, protect, and love unconditionally. It's no wonder so many parents don't know what to do with their lives once their children have grown up and have moved out of the nest to begin a path of their own. Alas, the empty nest syndrome kicks in and makes us all have to reacquaint with ourselves once again. It's funny in a sense of thinking that so many of us have lost a part of ourselves when we became parents. I mean really, how could we truly think that we could ever just disappear from who we truly are forever?

I believe that most of us actually forget just how much we are growing along with our children. It's hard to see it until we are no longer caring for them day in and day out. I imagine most parents consider each one of their children to be special. Of course, I felt that way too as everyone is special in their own unique way. However, to be completely honest, I always knew that my son was more than just a normal child. If you knew him, you would understand exactly what I mean. Each time I looked into his eyes, I could see that sparkle. He had a very sensitive heart as he could feel things that I was going through as if it were happening to him at the same time. The connection we shared was very strong and this continued throughout his life and only grew stronger when he became sick with cancer during the summer of 2002.

When my son Cody was born, Steven was ten years old. He was always asking me when he could have a little brother and he waited patiently for him to finally arrive. I think he thought Cody was his baby, his little angel to keep all for himself. The two of them were always laughing and just being silly, happy boys. Steven insisted that they share a room because he didn't want to be away from him. In the morning, he would take Cody from his crib and put him in bed with him, keeping him wrapped so cozy in his baby blanket. The abundant nurturing Steven shared with his brother was beautiful and it all came very naturally to him. He was this way with everyone. I've never known a child to adore another child so deeply. I have many photos of the two of them together. It's a good thing they both didn't mind posing for pictures. I find myself going through that massive box of photos a lot. I'll say this again, I wished I had the ability to paint so I could have captured my memories before they would one day fade away. To paint a picture, and try to capture the essence of Steven would have been like creating an image of a beautiful angel with magnificent, soft wings, sitting upon a large rock near the ocean surrounded by his brother Cody and many children, all basking in the warmth of his love and his nurturing energy. I can see him there now. In fact, I am sure that is exactly what he is doing now in heaven.

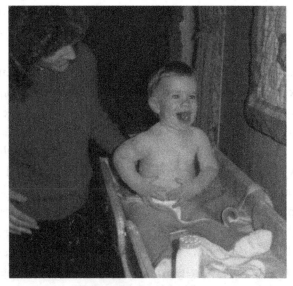

Steven absolutely loved baby powder!

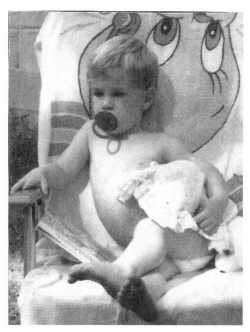

Steven loved his pillow and stuffed puppy, he carried
them around everywhere. This is one of my favorite
photos of him. It always makes me smile.

Hubbard Park. We absolutely loved going there to
feed the ducks and ice skate in the winters.

Fun in the photography studio trying out new backgrounds together.

Steven and his cousin Gary. They loved riding
the elephant and eating cotton candy!

We always had so much fun together.

More fun in the studio. We loved our bomber jackets - 1989

Company baseball game. Steven loved smiling for the camera.

Gramma and Grampa's 50th wedding anniversary party.

Our very first trip to Disney World together.
Just us two. We had a great time!

Fun World. One of our favorite places to hang out.
We took this just after riding the rollercoaster.

The Big Comfy Chair. We loved climbing up onto
this chair. We laughed the entire time.

Steven, Me and Baby Cody - August 9th, 1995

Steven and Cody - 1985

Steven adored his baby brother. His smile speaks volumes.

Steven, Cousin Allyssa, and Cody - the three musketeers!

Morning ritual. Steven loved it when Cody woke up
so he could put him in bed with him. So, cute!

Cody and Steven - brotherly love in Disney World.

Disney World - The Dolphin Hotel - we loved it there.

Steven and Cody - always laughing together.

Steven and Cody - playing in the snow.

Cody and Steven - their bedroom was their fun zone - all the time.

Cody and Steven - Catskill Game Farm, NY

Allyssa and Cody with Steven on his birthday.

Lake Winnipesauke in New Hampshire - they both loved the water.

Chapter 4

Senior Year

This is by far, the hardest, and most painful chapter for me to write. Today is March 20, 2010 and I am finally ready to begin this chapter. So much has happened in my life throughout this journey since Steven's death. I'll take you through the details of that later on. I simply just wanted to mention the date so that you'll know the significance of the time period in the creation of this story. Without knowing this, the rest will appear as if it were easily written. I assure you, it is never easy to put such a time in one's life into writing without feeling the pain all over again, reliving every single moment as if it were happening all over again. This was certainly a time full of turmoil and such deep, deep, pain for me to endure. I say this to you so that you will not read this chapter wanting to put this book down because it may bring up a lot of your own pain in which you may have kept buried deep inside. Please know that I never forgot any of those feelings, and I do know just how much it may hurt to read this chapter. This I can promise you, it will get better in time. All of it as you'll see. The next chapters will show you just how much better it actually became for me. If I can move forward in my life with a little less pain along the way, so can you.

Senior Year. This is supposed to be one of the most cherished moments in one's life. The last year of high school spent sharing some wonderful moments filled with laughter and numerous events shared with friends. All of whom look forward to a future filled with beautiful hopes and dreams.

Spending hours listening to music, being physically active, playing sports or to simply just watch friends play football and hanging out together afterward. These were the things that mattered most to Steven.

Being in high school, for most people, means enjoying every moment as if to capture it within their memory bank forever. To love freely, loving life, and seeing each day as a new adventure. Going to prom, staying out all night, making memories to last a lifetime and not having a care in the world. High school is the time to simply just enjoy life in every possible way. I believe that most eighteen-year-old boys feel that the sky's the limit and there is absolutely nothing else that really matters, right? Wrong. Oh, so very wrong. At least it was not meant to be this way for Steven.

The summer before Steven's senior year started out pretty normal. He spent a lot of time with his friends and his girlfriend. Life was fun for him, full of hope, talking about college and the dreams he had for his future. He was so excited about being on the football team and he took such good care of himself, both inside and out. He loved working out, eating all the best foods not only for his health, but also because he just absolutely loved food. This was not a new life style for Steven since he was always such a great athlete and loved to cook and experiment in the kitchen. He and I shared a great love of cooking and creating wonderful new dishes simply to just see our guests faces light up with delight after experiencing their very first bite. We did, however, keep our recipes a secret. We thought it was such an honor to be invited to a party with the request of bringing that special dish that only we could create. It gives me great joy today when someone asks me for one of those famous recipes. I simply smile and remind them that it's a family secret and cannot be shared, at least not yet.

I loved Steven's daily phone calls to my office asking me what we were having for dinner. This memory makes me smile as I reminisce in such moments because he really didn't want to know what I had planned to make for dinner. What he really wanted to know, however, was if he could request something that he liked, knowing that I would always make whatever he wanted. Since I began my love of cooking when I was just ten years old, absolutely loving every moment of experimenting with so many ingredients, naturally, Steven was much the same. Only he started out learning to cook by age four. He was always dragging his kitchen chair across the floor to get closer to the counter to help me. He constantly asked me a million questions while I taught him how to cook. We shared this love of gourmet food; magical smoothie concoctions; decadent desserts, secretly spiced buffalo wings, and so much more, including many other indulgences like sharing a cigar on special occasions; and listening to a vast array of music. In our home, music and cooking went together like peanut butter and jelly. *Bob Marley* was a favorite of ours and we played his greatest hits CD all the time. There is nothing better than listening to music and singing while in the kitchen creating something magical. At break time, we'd go outside and share a cherry or vanilla flavored cigar. Sometimes we would even share a *fatty*, a *Romeo and Juliet*, *Cohiba*, or a *Cojimar* vanilla, sugar-tipped cigar. I always loved the conversations that took place between just the two of us during those moments together. It was a very special bonding time. Just me and my beloved baby boy.

In August of 2002, Steven began not feeling well. I thought he was pushing himself too hard with his work-outs while he was preparing for the fall football season. I told him to rest more. He said he was exhausted all the time and could not get enough sleep as it was. He had flu-like symptoms accompanied with a sore throat and swollen glands. This was just the beginning of what was to come next. I will never forget the day he was lying on the coach watching the cooking channel, when he asked me to come feel the lumps he had in his groin, under his arm, and in his neck. We thought it was just swollen lymph nodes. And yet we both were concerned, I could see it in his eyes. The doctor said it was possibly viral and ran some tests. Within days, Steven was back at the doctor's office for more blood work. It all happened so fast. Virus one week, biopsy surgery the next. The diagnoses came like a tidal wave. Steven had cancer. Since some of the tests took longer to come in, we were hopeful that it was just a form of *Non-Hodgkin's Lymphoma* as the doctors said it might be. In most cases, this form of cancer has a much higher percentage for being cured with the proper treatment. The doctor told us the stains they were waiting on would diagnose the details pertaining to the non-curable kind of cancer, the kind that resides within the blood stream. The kind that we were hoping Steven did not have. We all prayed this would come back negative. However, that was not meant to be.

Steven did have cancer in his bloodstream. He had a very rare form of cancer. So, rare, that the doctors shared this in a national magazine later that year. It was diagnosed as, *Antiplastic Large Cell Lymphoma with Small-Cell Variant*, which is a form of *Non-Hodgkin's Lymphoma*. This particular form of cancer we soon learned has no cure. We prayed for a miracle and vowed to not let our fear take over our hope.

I don't think that any other thought went through my mind at that moment other than to ask the doctor what his plan was for treating my son and just how soon we could begin. It was at that very moment that Steven looked up from the game he was distracting himself with on his cell phone, that our eyes met, and I knew that he took comfort in knowing that I was going to make sure that we did whatever it took to make him better. I felt numb, and yet a strong motherly protection force kicked in. I was his mom, and he was my baby, and he was part of me, and I was ready to take on the world fighting for his life, and fighting for mine as well. We were connected, he and I, and no matter what was to come next, I was determined that we would do whatever it took to make him better. I would have done anything to see his beautiful face smile again, a smile full of happiness without this ugly illness threatening to take over his very existence.

Steven was seventeen at the time and I knew that he just wanted to go and be with his friends after we left the doctor's office that day. I knew that whatever was to come next, he had to live a normal life while the treatment was progressing, and no matter what, I would make sure this happened for him. I guess I did not expect that suddenly, I would feel like the whole world was crashing down on me once I was in alone and driving in my car. Suddenly, I just could not breathe. I was hysterical and cried the hardest I ever had in my entire life. I have never felt such an incredibly deep pain ever before. It came in like a tidal wave and there was nothing I could do to stop it. So, I did my best to get it together and drove myself to the office to gather my laptop and paperwork and let everyone know that I would be out for a while. I didn't know what else to do. I guess I thought I needed to at least try and keep life as normal as I could for all of us.

I left the office and headed home. About fifteen minutes into the drive, I simply just could not breathe. I lost all feeling in my arms and my legs. My entire body felt like it weighed a million pounds. All that heaviness was threatening to push me into the ground and it completely crushed me with no way to take in even the tiniest breath of air. I tried to breathe and push away the fear, but I could not control it. For the first time in my life, I just could not control my emotions. I lost it completely. I cried so hard that my tears were clouding my vision. I had to use every ounce of strength left within me to pull the car over on the highway. What a scary thing to do, pulling over on any highway filled with so much pain and being completely alone all at the same time. I told myself that this was it, no more tears. I let them all out, and I knew that it was time to pull it together and take care of my son and our family. I knew in my heart that it was going to be a rough road and I was so afraid. I was even more afraid of what the outcome might be, so I pushed that thought far away so it could not get a grip on my heart and soul.

Later that night, I went to bed hoping that I would fall asleep and find some sense of peace so that I could rest, and hopefully not wake up with the panic and abundant sense of fear that I had felt all day long. The dreams began, and the very first thought that came to my mind was, *Oh My God, my worst nightmare is here and it is very real. Is this why I felt that I could not see his life past high school? Is this it?* Whenever we talked about the future and college, my chest always felt so tight. I pushed those feelings away as quickly as they came. I only wanted to think of him today and prayed that he would be okay and that his life would continue just as it was meant to. There just had to be nothing that could ever get in the way of him being healthy and happy. He was an angel, remember? This could not be happening to him, not to this special young man who loved so deeply, so easily, and so completely. I refused to think in any other way, no way. He was going to be fine, perfectly fine. He just had to be.

And so, began the journey to wellness. There was no way to see it other than that. His journey... My journey... Our journey. We were always so close, so connected to one another. I could feel him, his emotions, his pain, his fear, his love, and his life. It radiated within me, it has always been this way. I thought that if I were strong and positive, then he would feel that, and it would help him to stay strong and positive too.

Treatment began right away as there was absolutely no time to waste. The first week was a horrific nightmare I am sorry to say, and trust me on this, I am not exaggerating one teeny tiny bit here. It was a horrific, extremely painful time, horrific for him, thus equally as horrific for me. Whatever he felt, I took into my heart and soul as well. He had a port put into his chest to receive the chemo that was meant to kill the cancer cells. He was aggressively ill immediately after receiving the very first dose of chemo. Shortly after they hung the first bag of chemo medicine, he began throwing up so violently that he could not make it to the bathroom, let alone the basin placed next to him on the side table. Almost immediately his beautiful blond hair started coming out in clumps. It was hell to watch and not be able to do anything to make it better for him. I literally watched my son go from being a very healthy teenager, to looking like an aged old man, so pale, so fragile, with no energy left in him whatsoever. Those beautiful blue eyes of his looked at me with great hope, and it was at that moment that I knew we were on the right path. The emotion in his eyes took my breath away every time he looked at me. I felt my heart beat with so much love for him and I knew he could feel it. Ever since I can remember, he and I shared this gift with one another. It was a gift, our gift, a beautiful gift. I will forever be thankful for that gift.

Some days were a bit easier on him. I longed for those days as they were the ones he would ask for his favorite baby bubble bath and lotion. We had this connection, he and I, we loved to hang out and just talk about things, anything really, just a special connection time for us both to share alone. Whenever he took a bath, and it was always a long bath, he would get everything ready, filling the tub with his favorite bubbles, setting a towel on the toilet seat, closing the curtain and then calling out to me, "Okay Mom, you can come in now." So, I would sit on the toilet seat and he would lay back and open the curtain so that we could see each other's faces and talk. He often did the same thing to me when I was in the tub. I always looked forward to that knock on the door followed by him asking me if he could come in and hang out. We shared so much love for each other, much more than just a mother and son. It was a blessing.

One day when I arrived at the hospital after work, Steven had a friend visiting. Her name was Laura; she had stopped by with her friend and her mom to say good-bye to Steven as she was leaving the hospital to go to a hospital in Boston for a different type of treatment that she could only receive there. She was around his age I guessed. Something made me really take notice of her and to hold onto the memory of her. I remember her smile and her kindness toward my son. They met during the time she stayed there. This made me happy because in the beginning, he was angry and didn't want to see anyone, let alone make any kind of friendships. That same week I also met a sweet volunteer named Erica. She had beautiful, long blond hair and a smile to match it. She was very warm and loving to Steven and I knew as soon as I saw them through the window that they had become friends. I remember arriving that day with his girlfriend and the look on her face showed her jealousy. I smiled to myself. Of all times to feel bad or to feel any sort of jealousy seemed so silly in the grand scheme of things. However, I understood. We said hello before Erica left. She said she was heading back to school and said how happy she was to meet me. I loved all the people that made my son's hospital stays pleasant. To play games with, watch movies with or just to hang out and chat were the little things that kept his life balanced and not so focused on the treatment at hand. At least that's what I hoped it did for him. And boy did he love to watch movies; we always did this together as well. We could never get enough of that. Music and movies. It was our special time to share.

Days turned into weeks, and weeks turned into months. During this time while in the hospital receiving round the clock treatment, we watched a ton of movies. We ordered all the foods that Steven loved, anything he wanted, anything to help him to be more comfortable. The treatment continued to be quite brutal most days. He was just so damn sick it broke my heart. Sometimes we had a couple days at home after treatment in which he felt good and could hang out with his friends, but this time period was always very short lived. He could never make it past an hour or so without having to go right home to bed. Around Christmas time, we went to the hospital so Steven could have a PET scan to see how the treatment was working for him. I was in the scan room with the doctors. This meant a lot to me as a parent, to be allowed to view the scans while the doctors explained everything they were seeing on the screen. They told me the scans were clear, yet they could not understand why I wasn't excited. I smiled a polite little smile, yet I did not feel their words to be true. Hopeful words, yet nothing more. I just knew something did not feel right.

I waited in a private office with the doctors while Steven got dressed. They wanted to share the good news with him as soon as he came to meet us. I am sure they thought I was in shock, otherwise how else could they explain my calmness, and then, there he was, my beautiful baby, walking through the door to that small office, looking very nervous as if the worst news was about to be shared. The doctors told him that the cancer was gone, the tumors were gone, and the scans were clear. Steven just looked at me and smiled. It was a beautiful hopeful smile. I smiled in return, allowing his feelings of hope to connect to my heart so that I could feel it too. We had a shot at this, or so we had hoped. We both knew that we could not think of anything other than living life with complete hope and faith that this would all be over soon. I also knew that both our smiles were not filled with joy. He knew exactly what I did, that this was far from being over. Only neither of us ever said it. I think we both probably felt that if we said it aloud, then we would make it become true. Then one day, he said he did not believe them. I told him to please focus on faith and positivity.

About four weeks after the scans, Steven became very sick, the lumps were all back, and he was feeling much worse than before. We were on our way back to the hospital for more tests. The doctor confirmed that the cancer was back and his lymph nodes were full of lumps once again. He said, "See mom, I told you they were not gone, I knew it." All I could do was to hug him and tell him that he needed to have hope.

The following months came with much more aggressive chemo sessions of which I thought Steven would not survive, as if the last few months were not strong enough chemotherapy, this time around was even worse. His health suffered tremendously throughout this time and that scared me to death. This treatment left him with little time to feel anything other than sickness and so much pain. My heart just broke for him. I wanted it to all just go away, but it had other plans and refused to let up. While Steven tried to be as normal as he could on his days away from the hospital, his energy was just not there. It took months for him to be able to get his driver's license because he was too weak to leave the couch, and since his white cell counts were always so low, we spent a lot of time in the hospital so he could receive blood transfusions and platelets. On the good days, I saw glimpses of my son, the one who always made everyone laugh. I was so thankful for those days. He even spent a lot of that time back then visiting the children in the hospital, and making the nurses laugh simply by just being Steve.

One night as I was lying in bed, I had the most overwhelming feeling of sadness and fear come over me. Only it wasn't coming from within me. I felt Steven's energy with me, all around me, within me and I knew it must be him. I got out of bed to put my clothes on planning to race to the hospital when I heard the house phone ringing. It was the middle of the night so I knew it had to be someone from the hospital calling. Oddly enough, I didn't feel panic so I answered the phone calmly. Sure enough, it was a nurse calling to tell me that Steven had been crying for a long time and he didn't want to talk to anyone or receive any medicine to help him sleep. She did tell me that he told them not to call me and to just leave him alone. After hours of this behavior, he finally agreed to allow them to call me. When I got to his room, he was laying on his side facing towards the windows. He didn't hear me, nor did he see me when I entered his room. I quietly put my things down onto a nearby chair and slipped off my shoes and climbed into bed with him so I could hold him. He looked up to see who it was and as soon as he saw my face, he just let the tears flow. I held him till the sobbing stopped and he fell asleep. I massaged his back like I did when he was little. Every night after we read a story in bed, he would lift his nightshirt and ask me to tickle his back. The tickle was actually just my finger tips creating soft feather strokes up and down his back. He loved that. I loved it too. In the morning when he awoke, he told me he was fine now and wanted to watch a movie with his friend in the other room. He told me that I should just go home and get some rest. Then he smiled and said, "Can you bring me El Sombrero's for dinner tonight?" I laughed and said, "Of course." He and I were much alike. We always tried to make the best of everything, no matter how bad or sad it may have been. A trait I admired in him and I'm sure he felt the same way about it himself.

Steven was too sick to go to school so he was appointed a tutor. She came to visit him in the hospital and even though I know how much he hated that, I knew we had to make sure it continued, as it was important to him to be able to graduate with his friends. I just wanted him to have some normalcy throughout this time. Some days he was healthy enough to attend school and even an occasional football game. He tried to hang on, and push through, but even after just a short half hour, his body fought him. I was just as disappointed as he was when he had to come home and rest. He kept fighting, but I knew it was taking a toll on him. He came home one day with his wrists all scratched up and when I asked him what had happened, he told me it was scratches from working on his car with his cousin. I knew by his face that this was a subject to let go of, as he was not going to tell me the truth.

I was beginning to feel afraid for him and his wavering strength. He said he was tired of all of it. I knew what really happened and why he wanted to give up on his life. We spoke to the doctor and tried new medications that would hopefully make him feel better, anything to help him get through this time with some sense of peace. It seemed to help, at least for a little while. Or so I thought.

One day while Steven was in the hospital, he was very upset when I arrived. He was on the phone with his girlfriend and he said he heard a guy's voice in the background. He thought there was someone at her house with her. He threw the phone down and left the room. When I picked up the receiver, I heard her crying and calling out to him, and then I heard the male voice, it was like a party line, with another conversation being held in the background. This is what he had heard. I calmed her down and told her that I was going to bring him back to his room and after he calmed down, I would have him call her. I found him down the hall from his room at the nurse's station. I explained the telephone situation to them. The nurses confirmed that this happened a lot.

Steven went back to his room and agreed to call his girlfriend before he got back into bed to rest. After they spoke, he quickly fell asleep, so I took a walk to the café to get coffee and some treats for him. When I got back to his room, he was not there. He had unhooked himself from his IV pole and left. The nurses and I looked everywhere. I panicked and was so worried as I knew he had almost zero white blood cells at this time and he also did not have any healthy blood platelets that would help his blood to clot if he were hurt in any way. The doctor was called right away, as was security. They sent out an alarm hospital wide, and shut down all the doors, including the entrances and exits. No one could get in or out. As panicked as I was, I just felt that he was okay so I started to feel anger towards him for doing this to everyone in the hospital. I thought of all those children and their parents worrying about what the hell might be happening. All because my son lost his temper and caused this major commotion.

About twenty minutes later, the doctor came into Steven's hospital room and said that he was found outside smoking a cigarette on the bench near the entrance. The security guards found him but he refused to go back in until he could speak to his doctor. So, his wonderful doctor had to leave his extremely busy, oncology office, full of sick children, to sit with Steven, and talk him into coming back inside. Steven told him that he did not want to do this anymore. He told him that he had had enough. Whatever the doctor said helped, as he finally agreed to go back to his room and finish the treatment. When he walked into the room, he had that smug, smirky, little smile on his face which thoroughly pissed me off. He said, "Hi Mom," and climbed back into bed. The nurses came in, gave him some medicine, and hooked him back up to his IV lines, as he quickly fell asleep. I took a walk outside to clear my head. I could not even speak to him at this point, as I was so mad. I knew I needed to calm myself down before we spoke.

When he woke, I reminded him of his selfishness, and that everyone was so panicked and worried, and that no one could get in or out because he had to get out and take himself to the gas station to buy a fucking pack of cigarettes. He smiled and said, "Chill Mom, it's all good, everything is fine now." Really? I was so pissed. It took all I had not to lose my shit, and scream at him at this point. Thinking back on this moment, all I can do is smile. I can hear his voice speaking these words to me and I totally get where he was coming from. This kid, my beautiful son, always had a way of making me laugh, and not take things too seriously. I miss the essence of him and hearing his voice and laughter every day. He was the light in my life.

In May of 2003, Steven spent an entire week in the hospital receiving blood and platelets so that he could attend his senior prom. I was so excited for him. He went with his friends to pick out his tuxedo and flowers. I wanted to make sure he had something very special for his girlfriend as she was a sweetheart and was with him along this entire journey. I loved her like my own daughter then and still feel the same way today. Steven spent an entire day cleaning and waxing his car for the prom. He just loved that car. The *Make a Wish Foundation* gave him a wish of his choice and he chose a stereo system complete with DVD player, alarm system, and an amplifier with subwoofers that would send his music blaring for miles. When the foundation first approached him, he told me that he did not want anything. He said that there were so many children who had nothing and they would never get the chance to become a man like himself. He said he already had a long life and that he wanted to give his wish to another child. I was so proud of him and his love of children and at that moment, I knew he was happy with himself as well. The foundation told him that all the children would get a wish, and that this was his wish, and they wanted him to have one just for himself. He wrote down a few ideas, all of which he could not do since his illness prohibited him from travelling, so after much thought, he chose to turn his beloved car, a 1995 dark green Acura Integra, into a glorified street machine, inside and out. It was a gift all its own and he was elated.

Steven, Ian, and Gary with Steven's beloved Acura
Integra - Senior Prom - May 2003

Me and Steven - Senior Prom - May 2003

Steven Thomas in his special outfit for the prom. I always loved the way he followed his own lead and dressed as he wanted to. This is one of my most favorite photos of him. One I keep close by always to remind myself of the passion and zest he had for life.

Steven had a great time at the prom celebrating with all his friends and teachers. Much of this evening has been captured on film, and for this gift, I am truly thankful. I was so happy that he stayed out for hours and seemed fine when he came home. Sure, he was a little tired, but nonetheless, he was feeling good, and this was glorious.

The good days lasted through much of the summer and then July came, and boy did it come with a vengeance. We spent a lot of time at Yale so that Steven could receive a stem cell transplant. This was to be the end of the blood cancer cells. The cells were clean, and the scans were clear and we were on to the next road to wellness. This was a tough time for him. He did look forward to going for treatments at Yale as he said he got to see *his girl*. She was an amazing woman who gave the patients massages. As she was a very loving person, I am sure her massage therapy treatments were equally as nurturing. Steven said that those were the best days. They were the only days that he felt relaxed and could sleep. After the stem cell treatment was done, the quarantine lasted for much too long, and it was hard on him being so sick with this aggressive form of treatment.

Steven had a tough time keeping his spirits up. A nurse arrived daily to give him his treatments, which only added to his depression. It seemed as if he was losing hope. I prayed for a miracle. Then one day, the road hit a major bump and Steven was back in the hospital. Only this time, he put himself there. He had given up and slit his wrists. I was terrified and angry at the same time. When I got to the hospital, he had that smug, little, smirky, smile on his face and I just absolutely lost it. I told him that he could never give up, and that he had to fight and to be strong and that if he gave up and took his own life he would never know what life he could have had. I reminded him of how special life was, and that it was a gift that was not meant to be tossed away like garbage. He yelled at me and said that I did not know what he was going through, and that I had no idea how he felt. I just about screamed these words to him, "Don't you see it, don't you know how much I love you and how much we are connected? That I feel what you do and that when you hurt I feel that pain and that I would do absolutely anything to take it from you and put it in me so that you could live a long and happy life?" His eyes never left mine, and from that moment on, I knew he heard me, and he knew exactly what I was talking about. I knew he felt it too and he then knew what he had to do. I prayed for a miracle. I prayed that he would have the strength to get through this ordeal. He just had to.

Steven had slit his wrists at his girlfriend's house. Her parents, as expected, were very upset about it so they called the police and had a restraining order put on Steven. They even went so far as to call me to say that if he ever went anywhere near her again that they would have him arrested. I was sick. These two loved each other so much. My son was far from being a person who would ever hurt another human being or any other living thing. I tried to see it from their perspective, but it just made no sense to me. I told her mother that they loved each other, and if anything, they were very close friends, and that they were together before the cancer came, and that she was there with him through it all. I asked her how she could see it in such an ugly way. She said they were not backing down and were quite serious with their threats. So, I told her that I would fight fire with fire. I reminded her that her beloved daughter was in love with my son as he was with her. It was a consensual relationship and that I did not respect, nor did I honor, her point of view, and that if she pushed through with her threats, I would make a case against them for harassment, especially since my son was so sick. He did not deserve to be treated like a criminal. I was so angry and I refused to back down. So, she said, "Please keep your son away from my daughter." I replied, "This goes both ways. She keeps calling the house, so this is on her too." She responded by hanging up the phone without saying another word. The emotion I felt at that moment far exceeds any sort of anger, trust me. I was beside myself. A feeling I have never, ever, felt before. I pray I never feel this way ever again. It was much too ugly.

Time went by and I knew that they were still seeing each other. It was very hard on them, and how could it not be. So, one day, her aunt called the police, and told them that Steven was coming around again. He didn't know there was an arrest warrant out for him. Shortly after that, Steven was at his cousin's house, just around the corner from her house, and the police came, and he was arrested. Can you imagine? This kid was so sick at this time. I called a family friend and we went to bail him out. I was so angry when the police officer came out sharing with me his attitude filled greeting. I immediately ripped into him about how sick my son was and explained the situation. He backed down, and we took Steven home.

Words cannot express my worry, fear, and anger, at this time. A time that was quickly showing signs of nothing good to follow.

A few days later, we went to the courthouse. Steven had a fever so I prayed we could take care of this situation right away so I could get him to the hospital. I spoke to a very nice woman in the clerk's office. I explained the situation. She took one look at my son and asked me for the doctor's phone number so she could verify his illness and try to push the case to another date. It was moved to the end of September. That woman was surely a guardian angel. I was so thankful for her help. I was also quite thankful to get the hell out of there. So was Steven.

Later that day, Steven was back in the hospital again as he was sick with a fever and needed blood transfusions and more platelets. Eventually he came home and he lived. He laughed, and he ventured onward as best as he could. He spent a lot of time at his friend's house, swimming, riding quads, and relaxing by the fire pit. He even went camping the following Labor Day weekend. Life was good, and it was moving onward. Steven was happy and he had faith that he was going to be okay. He was fighting for his life and he was living it, just the way he wanted to. He talked about going to college and becoming a nurse practitioner as he said he really wanted to work with the kids as he could relate to them and how they were feeling having been in their shoes himself. I told him that he could be whatever he wanted to be. He said he loved to cook too but he didn't want that as a profession as he felt he would not be able to be home with his family since chefs worked evenings and weekends often with very long hours. He said he'd rather just continue to cook for the love of it. This made me smile. My son was planning for his future. This just had to mean good news. This just had to mean he was going to be okay. This happy time was quite short lived.

While Steven was away camping over Labor Day weekend, he got sick with a high fever and had to go to the hospital. He had an infection, and he also had shingles. The doctors told us that one of the main concerns they had with having a stem cell transplant was that the body would no longer have any immunity, and with that, the chances were high for patients to get sick with viruses that the weakened body might not be able to fight. This was a nightmare. I thought he was doing better. He looked so good. He was my son again. I just wanted him to get better, hadn't he suffered enough? No matter what the doctors tried, he was just not getting any better. He was coughing up a very thick, black mucous, and it was taking away his entire being. By the third week of September, Steven woke up one morning unable to breathe. I remember that morning as if it were yesterday. I did not sleep very well the night before so my senses were extra heightened. I just felt that the morning was going to bring about a turn of events in a tough way for Steven and for our family. I stood there for what seemed like hours with my hand on the door handle to his bedroom, I was so afraid to open the door and see him in such pain. Then, I heard his labored, breathless, voice call to me. He said, "Mom, I can't breathe, can you take me to the hospital now? And mom, please don't call an ambulance, let's just drive there, I'll be okay."

I had to dress his weak body and help him get up the stairs. His little brother Cody was panicked by seeing his brother in this state. I told him it was going to be okay and that I had to get him to day care so he could get to school and that we would see him later that day when he got home. I was doing my best not to show my fear. Believe me, I will never, ever, forget that moment as long as I live. There is nothing worse than seeing your child so sick, and so full of fear, knowing that your loving embrace and kisses cannot take the fear or illness away.

Labor Day Weekend 2003 - Steven absolutely loved riding quads.

Labor Day Weekend 2003 - Steven enjoying the weekend with his friends.

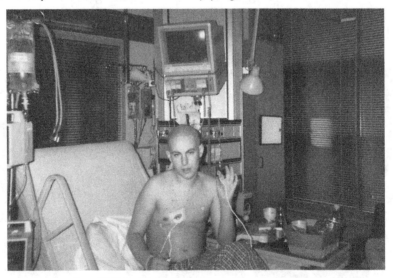

September 2003 - Just after Labor Day Weekend - this is
the very last photo ever taken of my beautiful son.

September 2003 - Steven thought it was funny that he had a "backup" toilet in his room. It's things like this that always made him laugh.

Twenty minutes later, we made it to the hospital and they were waiting for us at the entrance with a wheel chair. I watched them wheel my son away while I raced to park the car. It seemed like forever before I found an available spot. I literally ran to the hospital entrance and had to wait to go through security before running to the elevator. Panic seized me. It wrapped itself around my heart and lungs. I repeated the same phrase over and over again in my mind, "Oh God, please, please take care of my son until I can get there." When I got to his room, there he was, sitting in a chair with the oxygen mask covering his very pale face. He looked up at me with those blue eyes of his full of exhaustion, tired of it all, yet he looked at me as if asking me to help him. I will never forget that moment, or the pain in his eyes, and the expression on his face. It was at that very moment that I felt more fear than words can ever express. Before they took him away to the ICU, he took the oxygen mask from his face and said, "Mom, whatever happens, don't let them take me to Yale. I want to stay here. And don't let them take out my brow piercing, it's too new and it will close up and I'll have to do it all over again." I smiled, and said, "Okay honey, don't worry, I won't."

When the doctor asked me to come with him, I knew by the expression on his face that this was not going to be good news. That hopeful face I knew so well for the last fifteen months was definitely not there this time and I did not want to hear anything other than what his next plan of treatment was. He said there was little oxygen getting into Steven's lungs and that they needed to get him onto a respirator as soon as possible so, they could help him breathe, and figure out what they needed to do to help him get better. Panic and fear gripped me in a way that I never knew I could feel. Yet there it was, suffocating me, pulling me downward onto a path that I was destined to walk upon. I have no idea how I was able to breathe on my own, let alone stand up and walk. I prayed that I would have the strength within me like never before to make it through this.

The next three weeks were exhausting, emotionally, mentally, and physically. My beautiful little boy lay before me covered in tubes full of medicine and oxygen. I stayed by his side doing everything I could to help keep him to stay calm and feel comfortable. I hated that he had to be on the respirator so deeply sedated so that he would stop moving around and trying to pull out the air tube. It was a very painful and devastating time and nothing was worse than seeing my son in such a state. Being so close to him and feeling the pain along with him was almost too much to bare and I did all I could to fight that pain with every single molecule of my very being. It took everything I had left within me to stay strong for him, for myself, and for Cody.

The biopsies revealed that the infection was growing within his lungs and the many various antibiotics that they were giving him did little to change this. Nothing was helping. Steven had no white cells left to fight the infection with, and he also had no platelets, which was a nightmare because of the bleeding it could cause internally with the oxygen tube in place. Any sort of movement he made only worsened this situation. All I wanted to do was lie by his side so I could hold him and soothe him just like I did when he was little. I found a chair that I could raise up high enough to sit close to him and be able to put my head on his pillow next to his sweet face. I gently laid my head next to his on the pillow, gently holding him close to me. It was only then that he would finally sleep. I washed his face and put lotion on his hands and feet, and when he was resting peacefully, I was able to put it on his arms and legs. It was his favorite baby lotion, the one that made him smell so clean and fresh just like when he was a baby. I kept the TV on all the time tuned into his favorite channels, *Nick at Night*, and *The Food Network*. I did everything I could to keep the room peaceful and quiet so he would be able to rest as peacefully as he could.

A couple of days later, the doctors removed Steven from the respirator to see how he would do on his own. He was in so much pain that the medication they needed to help keep him comfortable kept him extremely groggy and since his breathing was so labored, he just slept most of the time. He could not talk, or move. He was like a rag doll. He would open his mouth so I could feed him but it was not enough to sustain him for more than a half day so they had to put him back on the respirator. This made the protective walls around me start to crumble. Before they did this, I begged the doctor to wake him enough so that I could talk with him, but he said they couldn't do that as it would have been unfair to Steven because he was not able to breathe on his own anymore. I hated it. I wanted to scream out, "WHY my son, why is this happening to such a beautiful person?" It was hell and it hurt so much to see him this way. I refused to give up hope. Just before they asked me to leave the room so they could put him back on the respirator, I told Steven how much I loved him. His eyes were closed, but he pulled the oxygen mask down from his face and he said, "I love you too Mom." Those were the last words I heard my son speak. I will never forget that moment, nor the sound of his voice. It was a beautiful moment and I know it was his gift for me.

As if this time wasn't hard enough, at home, our basement flooded, as did his beautiful room that we built for him. This was something I was just not up for handling. At that time, I was grateful that my ex and his beautiful parents helped to clean up the water damage. Without getting into it, I just want to state, at this point, that he sort-of mentally and physically check-out. I am sure this was all too much for him to handle, so he did what he does best, bury himself in work and other things. I needed this situation handled so I called Kevin, my long-time family friend, my brother Ryan's best friend since the eighth grade, over to help. His family owns a cleaning company and he came right out to help remove the water and set up fans to dry out the carpet. Since the water was still coming in all we could do was lift the carpet and await the water to stop before it could be cleaned again. Kevin was very upset that no one had called him to tell him about Steven. He had known him since Steven was very little. They used to play football in the front yard together along with my brother. I felt thankful at that moment that he was there helping me. He was always so good to me and to my family. We all considered him as a part of our family.

That same day, I was at home, making calls to deal with Steven's court issue. If you think that going to court sucks, then trust me when I say this, trying to deal with these things over the phone is even worse, especially when you are trying to get this all done in an hour of time so that you can get back to the hospital ASAP. Although I am sure they receive many calls from those who might be considered, out of sorts, they did listen to me as I shared Steven's story and they asked me to have the doctor's office fax them a letter ASAP so they could put the case on hold until Steven was well enough to attend court. They then reminded me, with attitude I might add, that the restraining order still stood strong. Really? I simply thanked them for their help and hung up the phone, muttering under my breath, "Fuck you, you fucking assholes."

Kevin and his co-worker Matt came back upstairs and said they did all they could for now and Kevin asked that I contact Matt once the room was dry so he could come out and finish it and put everything back in place as Kevin was going to be away on his honeymoon. I hugged him good-bye and thanked him for going above and beyond to help me with this. Steven's room was very important to me as it needed to be in perfect, clean order, for his arrival home. I was thankful that nothing of Steven's was ruined. I was even more thankful that I had a friend like Kevin to help me in this time of crisis.

October 9th arrived, and Steven was having a rough time. He was bleeding internally and went into respiratory distress. I told him to stay strong and to keep fighting and that everything was going to be okay. He shook his head *No* and was trying to talk to me while still on the respirator. The nurse was in a panic as she said he should not be moving at all since they gave him enough medicine to keep his body completely paralyzed. She quickly left the room to get more medication to sedate him even more but I knew he was doing this for me. I started to leave the room to follow the nurse to plead with her not to give him any more medication and told her that he just needed me next to him, to help keep him calm. A family friend who was sitting with Steven called to me, crying, saying, "Dee... Dee... LOOK... he's calling you back to him with his hand." He used his finger to call me back to his side and he was trying to open his eyes to talk to me but nothing came out except his tears. My heart hurt so much. What was he trying to say? I stayed with him the whole time they were wheeling him down the hall to get a CT scan that they needed to determine the depth of the internal damage. I talked to him and that seemed to help him to relax a little. I stayed with him while the scan was in progress. He was quiet as long as I spoke to him and stayed by his side. When we got back to his room, he was asleep, unmoving. I told him that I missed him and that I just wanted him to get better so that he could open those beautiful blue eyes of his again and say, "Hi Mom" just one more time. At that very moment, he struggled with everything he had to force his eyes open. Even though it was just for a brief moment, it meant everything to me. It was then, that I knew he had been there with me the entire last three weeks, hearing every word, feeling every emotion. I had seen him cry a few times in his sleep so I often wondered what he was thinking about during those moments. One thing I did know for sure was that he knew that he was loved and that he was not alone.

On October 10th, Steven's lungs were filling with blood and the machines were doing all they could to keep his body alive. I continued to hold on to hope. After all, miracles could happen at any given moment, right? I prayed for a miracle. When Steven went into respiratory distress, the doctor said that they could not bring him back if it happened again. I knew they were trying to make us understand that it was time to let go, but I just could not bear that thought. I did not want to say good-bye to my baby. I just wanted him to get better. I wanted him to come home. I missed him so much.

I stayed by his side all night. I could not sleep and yet I knew he was not there. His body lay lifeless other than the machines keeping him breathing and keeping his body alive. I knew it was almost time. I cried and I put my head on his pillow next to him. I knew he was already gone and I knew I had to make some calls to get things prepared. When I started to leave his room, walking toward the door, I stopped, frozen in my steps. I felt him walking behind me. I felt him all around me. I turned to look back at him lying in the bed and it was at that moment that I knew he had left his body and he was with me. He followed me to the private room in which I kept my things during those last three weeks. I sat on the little couch and cried and I put my head on his shoulder as he sat there next to me. I have never felt so much peace, and so much love surround me, encompassing me in ways I never even knew existed. I knew he was there with me. He was helping me to stay calm through his transition. There is nothing more beautiful than witnessing your child being born but to also be with them upon their death is a whole other story. It was the most beautiful feeling. I so wish I could paint it. But then again, it is a beautiful painting within my mind just as it is.

I spent the rest of that night in his room watching the monitors show the life leaving his body. The respiratory nurse told him it was okay to go and not to be afraid as I held him close to me, stroking his face and head telling him how much I loved him and not to be afraid that Grammy Lois would be there waiting for him. I just knew she would be there. She loved him so much and I was so thankful that she was in heaven, waiting for his arrival. It gave me peace as I knew she loved him as I did and that he would never, ever, be alone, no matter where they were going to next. I trusted that with all of my heart and soul.

What a beautiful gift to experience in this lifetime. To have the gift of feeling my son still with me and then to feel him leave his body and cross over to a place I knew existed, yet still a place in which I have not yet quite figured out and still had no feelings about up until this very moment. I knew it was going to be beautiful for him, yet I worried about what it was going to be like for him without me. His heart stopped, and then the machines stopped, and then he was gone. I was so thankful for the time I had with him alone, just the two of us after he left his body. I wanted to bathe him, and dress him in his clothes and shave his face to get him ready for the funeral home. I wanted him to look the way he looked before he arrived there. I think he even tried to make me laugh while I was painting his hands with blue paint to make his handprints on paper, just as he did when he was little. They are beautiful mementos to cherish forever. I felt his hand pull away and I said aloud, "Steven. Stop it! That's not funny." I could hear his chuckle and it made me cry. I knew he was just trying to help me but after the last three weeks of suffering, let alone the last fifteen months of his illness, I could not really find much peace at this moment in time.

I wondered if I would ever find peace without him to share life with ever again. My ex cried and tried to hug me, but I pushed him away and said, "Not now, he needs me, and I need to be with him alone and clean him up. I'll see you later." I am sure my words were like a slap to his face but I did not mean them to be, I just wanted to be with my son and do what was needed to be done quickly before his body was no longer able to be moved around. The body quickly becomes cold and turns purple, unable to easily be manipulated almost immediately after death. At first that scared me but then I realized Steven was with me and not in his body any longer. The fear quickly dissipated. I was thankful for that. I remember walking down the hall that night and stopping for a moment as I felt frozen in place. I noticed a mother was in one of the rooms holding her baby girl. She was crying and at that moment I knew her little girl would soon be going home to heaven too. I heard Steven's voice say, "She is with me now Momma, she is my little girl now. I am taking good care of her." I felt the love in his voice, the pride that he was taking care of one of his beloved children. I wished I could have spoken to this woman but I knew I was not supposed to and that nature had to take its course for both of them just as it had for us. It made me sad and I prayed that she would find peace in her daughter's passing. So, I continued walking down the hall, on my way to the private room to gather my things and then go home.

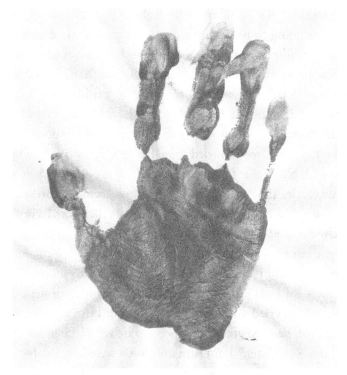

After Steven passed, the hospital helped me to make a handprint of his hand for a special keepsake.

I did not know how to say good-bye, or how to leave the hospital, the place in which we spent so much of the last fifteen months. I told the doctor that I did not know what to do next. He said that Steven was in good hands and that the funeral home would come to take his body away to prepare him for the services. He assured me that he would stay with him until they arrived. I knew it was just a body at this point, a shell in which held his spirit, his soul. I know this may be hard to comprehend, but it really is a magnificent experience to be with someone you love so much and witness their crossing over. It is so beautiful and I am so thankful that I did not miss a moment of it.

I have no idea how I made it out of the hospital and into the car. I think it was around 3am when I finally left to go home. I have no recollection of the drive home. I only remember that the peace was leaving me and that the grief, fear, and pain were settling in. Suddenly, I remembered how I felt when he was leaving his body. I felt him surrounded by so much love, light, and a beautiful sense of peace. The connection that a mother shares with her child, that beautiful bond, that *magical cord of light* connecting us to one another was cut away from me. He took it with him when he left me. I felt the warmth of him and the love of him float away. It left me with a huge black, gaping hole in my chest where my heart once carried so much love and peace. It was gone, he was gone, and my entire world fell apart. My baby would never again be coming home with me. The grief took over every single ounce of me and I had no control over it at all. And then it hit me hard when we pulled into the driveway of our house. Steven's car was parked in the driveway, in its usual spot, and I knew he would never be driving it again. His car, his beloved car. I hated seeing it knowing he would never again be pulling into the driveway, music blaring, ever again. I hated being home without him. I did not want to be home, I wanted to be with him. It hurt me so much to see it, like a blaring stop sign reminding me that everything here meant nothing anymore. My heart shattered into a million pieces. The pain was extremely debilitating.

I remember walking into my bedroom feeling so much devastation. My heart hurt so much. I was home and he was not. "Oh God, how could you take him now, he was only eighteen?" I was sick to my stomach, and I could not breathe. I dropped to the floor sobbing, feeling the pain encompass me, drowning me in a deep sorrow. I thought I was dying and I wished I were. It was at that very moment that Steven came, and he was not alone. Archangel Michael was there and he gently whisked me from the floor and laid me on the bed. I felt his massive wing span of soft, billowy, feathered wings, as they lovingly surrounded me in their embrace. He stayed with me, holding me close in his warmth and love. He kissed my forehead and brushed my hair from my face. I felt him hold me as Steven lay next to me on the other side. I fell asleep in this beautiful state of peace, surrounded by so much love and beautiful white light. I don't know how long I was there for, but I know it was a great gift that I will cherish always. I know it was Michael who brought Steven to me that day. They came together to help me get through the first big wave of grief so that I would know that I was never going to be alone again. It was in that moment that I knew Steven was my guardian angel and I also knew that my beloved Archangel Michael was, in fact, very real and his presence was, and will always be, perfectly, divinely, utterly, magnificent.

When I awoke the next morning, I felt like I was in a daze. I was exhausted, I had more emotions running through my body than I knew what to do with so I tried with everything I had to get myself up and get to the funeral home to make the arrangements in which to bury my son. The first thing I did was call his girlfriend, I wanted to go over to her house to tell her in person but I knew I could not see her parents after all they put us through with the police, nor did I trust myself with the things that I might say. It broke my heart to have to tell her that Steven was gone. And of all days, it was her sixteenth birthday. I told her that he died so that he could leave his body and be with her, to celebrate with her, on her special day. I prayed that would give her some comfort.

My beautiful sister Kim arrived shortly afterward to come clean the house for me, she didn't know what else to do but to help me by making things around me clean so I didn't have to do it myself. She is amazing at this, making things feel clean, and special. I really appreciated that. I remember asking her where my ex was. She said she didn't know, and that she had not seen him, so I just left and went to meet my Aunt Claire at the funeral home by myself. There is a heaviness that sets in when one has to make funeral arrangements for their child. As much as I was in such pain, it was so important to me to make sure that we chose everything perfectly suited to who Steven was. From the flowers, to the photo collages, the music, the words printed on the memorial cards, the casket, the clothes to dress him in, the memorabilia we just had to have with him in his casket, to the beautiful urn shaped like a beautiful temple in which to bury his ashes in, to the white doves for the burial. Everything had a special meaning. Every choice we made was just for him, to honor him. The funeral home staff was so kind and they helped so much. So much support was offered as they explained everything in great detail to us. I was so thankful.

After the funeral home, I went to see Cody. He was with family. He was so upset when I told him that his brother died. He cried and said with anger, "You said everything was going to be okay." I replied, "Yes I did.

And it is now honey. Now Steven is not sick anymore and he can be with us in spirit. You know he will always be with us, he told us that before he left, remember?" His little eight-year-old body ran to my arms and he cried. It was heart wrenching. I just prayed that we would be able to make it through this time and that we would actually be okay. It scared me to death.

When we returned to the funeral home for the calling hours the next day, I remember seeing my son lying there in his football jersey, showing off his beloved number nineteen, and the very first thought that came to me was, "Oh, that's not my son; it doesn't even look like him." When I touched him, I remembered how fast the body turns a purplish color when the oxygen has left it. The heavy makeup was necessary to give the body a flesh color. I knew that this was just his body, the vessel in which carried his soul. The true essence of him and who he was while he was here on earth was his spirit, his soul, and that no longer resided in this body that used to belong to him. I had peace at that moment knowing he was near, I could feel him next to me telling me it was okay and that he was not in his body anymore and that he was glad to be free of it finally. At that moment, it was still hard to believe that he was gone, yet I knew he was helping me to stay strong that day. The funeral home was jam packed with people. There were so many friends, and family members including the high school football team, co-workers, his coaches, teachers, and so many others that came to pay their respects. I was determined to stand there and be strong so that I could take in every word that was said, every experience these people shared with Steven were words that were music to my ears and to my ever-aching heart. Seeing some of his friends fall apart nearly did me in. Their grief was so intense; I could feel their pain when they hugged me. It tore my heart into pieces. I did not want them to feel that kind of pain. No one should have to feel that. Especially not at age eighteen. I stood there, embracing people, crying with some of them, trying to hold onto their words of love and admiration for my son. I was so thankful to them for doing this for him, for me, and for our family. All the while, my little Cody was by my side, holding my hand. His little face was so full of sadness it broke my heart. Steven's girlfriend came with her mother, but her mother waited outside in the car. This hurt me so much as this beautiful young girl needed support so I went to her; to hold her, and tell her that I loved her. I did not know what to do to help her except to tell her that she would always be like a daughter to me, and that she would always be part of our family, and that I would always be there for her.

I have little recollection of actually being asleep that night. I just remember waking early so I could be with Cody before we had to be at the funeral home. He was so young and I knew he was devastated. He and Steven were so close, so much in love with one another. I prayed this would not break his heart forever. He stayed by my side, his little hand gripping mine. My little man, he was so sweet and terrified all at the same time. We drove to the funeral home and we sat in the front row for the last viewing before leaving for the church services. I was numb. I knew the drive was short but it felt like an eternity. The day prior, I had given Steven's car to his cousin Gary. They were only four months apart and were always very close. I knew it was what Steven would have wanted. It made me so happy to watch Gary drive away with the car that the two of them spent so much time on, sprucing it up and enjoying the stereo system, while parading around town playing their favorite music in. I knew it was hard for him, but all I wanted was for him to love it and have fun with it like Steven always had. I guess I didn't expect to fall apart once they left the house that day, taking the car away from my home. To hear the music playing nearly broke my heart into oblivion.

I asked Gary if he would drive the car at the front of the funeral procession line, in front of the other cars and limos. I watched him get into the car the next morning along with his brother Michael. As soon as they started the car, I saw the look of shock on both of their faces. It made me rush over to them to see what was wrong. On the car stereo, in blue letters, it read, "See you soon." I said, "It's okay. That's meant for you. Steven is with you, you can do this honey. It's your car now. Enjoy it today and every day after this. Play his favorite song as loud as you want." And he did. After I got into the limo, I felt a little better. It made me happy to watch the boys, Steven's boys, get in line and lead the way behind the hearse. I know it must have been hard for both Gary and Michael to do this, but I do hope it meant a lot to them as well. Once everyone was in line we made the drive to the church. I was not expecting to drive by the high school where Steven went. To drive by during the weekday and see everyone outside, especially on the athletic field, just killed me. All I could think about was Steven and feeling that he should be there with them and not be here taking part in his own funeral. It sucked. I hated it. I was so angry and so devastated. Why him? Why now?

When we finally arrived, Cody and I made our way through all the people, sitting there, watching us walk down the aisle, their faces not hiding the sadness and pain they felt nor did they hide the pity that they felt for us as well. We sat in the front of the church and I could not get myself to look anywhere except at the casket that was right next to us. Watching my beloved family members carry the casket hurt so much to see. No more smiles on their faces, just sadness as if they could not believe they were there. What a thing to ask someone to do. I imagine it made them all proud in some sense, yet I am sure they also felt a little bit of fear as well having to be so close to the casket itself, and carrying what once was a very alive and beautiful person, one they loved and knew so well.

I heard every word the priest said, I felt the emotion coming from him and the emotions that were filling the entire church. It was a beautiful memorial service in honor of my son. The music was beautiful and perfectly selected, honoring him with words sung by a beautiful golden voice. An angel came to sing for him that day. Just for him. It was his sweet cousin Melanie. She sang her heart out. It was beautiful. I hugged Cody close to me, feeling his gentle spirit so close to mine. I was thankful for having him right there next to me. We needed each other. I felt so peaceful, surrounded by so much love and light, and then, I heard my name being called to come and give the eulogy. The speech that I had no way of writing ahead of time since I just could not put all of my thoughts and emotions into writing at that time. It was too much, there was a lifetime of things to say, moments to share, and so much love to express. My entire body felt like a bowl of jello, my legs were unable to steadily carry me and I prayed that I would find the strength to keep myself together. As soon as I stood there at the podium looking at all the people, I felt a wave of emotion cross over me like a tidal wave. So many had their heads hung low full of despair and tears for my son, others anxiously looked at me as if waiting for me to tell them something that would make them feel better, words from another place in time in which they could gather peace from. I have never seen so many people fill a church as I did on that day. I felt my legs begin to give out, my heart was pounding in my chest and I felt like I was going to fall to the floor, collapsing into a pool of tears. I asked for strength, I needed to do this for my son, there was so much to say and I wanted to honor him for who he was as a person, a human being, a very special soul, and then, he was there. I felt him holding me up and the peace took over my body. He said, "It's okay Mom, you can do this, I'm here with you, I am so proud of you. Thank you for loving me so much." Then suddenly, I found my voice and the words just flowed. I told the football team how much Steven loved being part of them and how special it was that they were all there dressed in their jerseys and their letter jackets. Each and every one of them was there to honor him. I talked of how beautiful and loving he was ever since he was born and how much he loved children and animals and how sweet he was and so full of love and how he took great pleasure in making people laugh. I talked about his kind heart and how it was so pure and sensitive. I talked about how he spent much of his time in the hospital visiting his little friends who were sick too. He loved that so much. Seeing the babies and talking so gently and lovingly to all of them. I talked about his life, from the beginning, to the end, and that gave me the greatest sense of pride. I was bursting with my love for him and I wanted everyone there to know just how very special he was so they would never forget him. He was here. His life had a purpose, his soul had a mission and a journey to be lived, he was a child of love, and that would never go away.

After the services were over, Steven's casket was wheeled to the entrance of the church. Once they got it into the hearse to bring him to the crematorium, the entire football team stood on either side of the hearse and as it was leaving the church parking lot, they all marched into a figure eight, an infinity symbol, before coming back together again. It was beautiful and I know Steven was watching them, feeling thankful that he was being honored in such a way. After that, we had a gathering in the meeting room of the church. It was nice to have some time to talk with so many people that day but I was antsy to leave and go home to where I felt safe and comforted with just my friends and family so we left shortly afterward to be with everyone there.

A few days later, Kevin and Matt came over to finish Steven's room. They made everything look new again. I was so happy to put everything back into its place so I could lie on his bed and smell his pillow and feel close to him. To look at all his things and stay close to him for a little longer. Before they left I remember looking at Kevin as he was standing in my kitchen. He was always so kind and loving to me. I had a thought cross my mind at that very moment, "He loves you, he's always loved you, you can trust him, and he'll always be there for you". Shortly after they left, I called him and was thankful that I received his voicemail and not actually him. So, I said the words I had always wanted to say, "Hi Kevin. I just wanted to say thank you from the bottom of my heart for always being there for me when I needed you and your help over the years. The countless times you have cleaned my carpets and other things that needed emergency attention and never charging me a penny. I don't call you because you do it as a gift; I call you because I trust you and don't ever want it to be anyone other than you. I always knew you had special feelings for me and loved me since we were kids. I wished I really knew the depth of that way back then because if I did, things would be very different today. Thank you for being you and for helping me make this day better. You have no idea how much you mean to me and how much your extra attention and support has been for me. Thank you so much. I really appreciate you." He called me shortly after and asked what I was doing that night and he then said that we should get together. And we did. I have never had so much fun. I felt like I was right where I needed to be, with my friend, the one who loved me since we were kids, the one who was there for me, to talk to, to laugh with, to be myself with. He was the only one that made me feel comfortable to be with at that time. I felt safe, I felt comforted, and I felt loved. We stayed out all night, just being in the moment, and I knew he was there for a reason. At that time, I still had no idea what was coming next, only I did know it was not going to be easy.

In the morning, my ex said, "You got home late huh? I'm so glad that you have someone to be there for you." I could only respond by saying, "Yes. Kevin has always been a very special part of my family since he and my brother met when they were in the eighth grade. I've known him for a very long time. He's always been a really good friend to me." He said, "Good. I'm glad." And he left for work. I was not really mad that he was not really present for me through all of this. I didn't really blame him for mentally checking out as I knew he had to deal with Steven's illness and loss as best as he could. But I did feel isolated and alone and I did feel my walls coming up to protect myself for the end that I knew was about to come. In the beginning, I had cried and asked him to please not leave us. He responded by saying, "Why do you say that? If anything, this will make us even stronger as a family." I just *felt* it coming. I felt the devastation coming, I cannot explain it. I just *knew* it.

I don't remember the next few days after that, I only remember the day in which we held the private burial ceremony. It was not too long after the church services but it felt like a lifetime to me. I remember standing at Steven's gravesite, a beautiful place in an oak tree-filled cemetery, a place where my beloved Grammy Lois was buried. We had a special granite head stone made for Steven, one that matched my grandparents. Steven's urn was to be buried on top of Grammy Lois's site. His stone was placed in the ground in front of the large standing family stone. It looked beautiful with all the flowers planted in front of it. It gave me comfort in knowing that he was so close to her, not only in heaven, but also in this memorial site. So many people came. It was so beautiful. My father and his wife came, and I was so thankful to see him there. It hurt me to see the pain on his face. My mother was standing behind me. I heard her say in a seething voice, "What the hell is HE doing here?" I turned around and said to her, "I asked him to be here, he is my father and Steven's grandfather. Get a hold of yourself or you can leave". I didn't want to hurt her but it pissed me off that her hatred for him just had to be shared on this day, of all days. It was quite selfish I thought. It's hard to understand this concept when one is burying their child. I had zero patience for it, and I didn't think I should have had to make allowances for it either on this day.

Shortly after, a very kind man gave us white doves to be set free to honor Steven with. They gave them to Cody and me and to Steven's father and Steven's other siblings. My mother interrupted the man in an annoyed, angry tone of voice saying, "Excuse me! This CHILD does NOT have a dove." She was referring to my niece Lissa. I turned around, once again, to address her and her actions and said, "Mom, please, the doves are for the parents and the siblings only. Just stop it!" The man was so kind; he touched my arm and said, "It's okay, I have extra." And he gave one to my niece and to anyone else who asked for one. I just wanted this moment to be peaceful, to have a burial for my son surrounded in love and peace. I really could not handle much more. I guess I was foolish in thinking that the family drama would be a thing of the past at this time. It saddens me that so many cannot put themselves and their issues aside at such an occasion. Once the services were complete, I walked with the funeral director to his car to get Steven's clothes and shoes that I had dressed him in after he had died in the hospital. I took the bag and put it into my car before we all left to go home.

Once we got home, the food was already being set up, and many of Steven's friends were arriving. I loved this. I always loved having them over my house whenever they came to hang out with Steven. It gave me comfort. The first thing I did was to take Steven's clothes out of the bag and put them into the closet where the hamper was. My dog Kelsey was right there; she got in front of me to sniff his clothes and would not stop until I told her it was okay. She adored her Steven. It broke my heart to watch her do this. She looked up at me and slowly walked away to go lay in her bed. I put his hospital blanket in her bed with her so she could smell him and hopefully find some comfort in that. I am sure she felt him with her, as she never left his side when he was home. We called her *nurse nana* like the dog in *Peter Pan*. She always took such good care of her beloved family. This feisty, yet very sweet little Jack Russell Terrier came into our lives and brought so much love. She never looked for Steven to come home again after that day. The red sweatshirt he was wearing had some mucous on it, it must have come out after he was dressed in it on his way to the funeral home. This did not make me feel sad or upset. It must have been there for her to smell so that she could make peace with his departure in some kind of way. At least that's what I told myself.

Steven and his beloved Kelsey - July 9, 2003

Chapter 5

The Grieving Process

How does one move on with their life upon the burial of their child? I bet you're asking yourself that question right now. Believe me, unless you've actually lost a child of your own, you cannot even begin to imagine what it feels like. There is nothing else to compare it to. It's funny, so many people feel that it must be easy when they know you have other children at home that need you or maybe you have a spouse who loves you so much that it must make it all that much easier to get through such a time. Family is always there too, right? Well, trust me when I say this, death is all consuming, encompassing your entire being with so much pain, so much heartache and complete emptiness and utter devastation. It does not allow you one single moment to breathe in peace while you are in the grieving stage which appears its ugly self in a much different depth shortly upon the actual burial of your child. It would be an understatement if I said that time heals everything. No matter how many children a person has at home, it does not diminish the pain of losing just one of them. Nor does it make you feel better knowing you have other children to care for either.

I was so amazed at the way people told me how I should grieve. That I had to let it out and to take medication, saying that it would help me. This just makes me laugh because no matter how hard I tried to tell them I just wanted to be left alone, they refused to let me just BE. I couldn't be there for my family to help them with their grief. I could barely keep my mind focused on staying together to just get out of bed every day. Since my son lost his life to cancer, I can tell you honestly that it is not better to lose someone you love in this way. So many people have thought that if you get to say good-bye, then it makes it easier to do so. I have many friends that have lost children in so very many other ways, and they all feel the same despair that I do. Is it really all that much different a feeling to lose a child quickly in a tragic death due to an accident, a suicide, or a murder? Imagine all the other feelings that those parents live with having to go through such a painful form of loss. I think of them all having witnessed myself, Steven's own attempts at checking-out early. It does not change the depth of pain if their children have died in utero, stillborn, age two, ten, fifty, and so on and so forth. It's still a nightmare to have your child pass away before you do. It's a natural feeling to want to embrace your children throughout their lives. It's only when we are old that it's okay to cross over right? It's the ultimate dream. The natural order of life, right? To marry and have a family and to find or build the perfect home, the many fun filled vacations, growing old with our children and grandchildren. At least that's what I wanted for my life. So, who's to say what the best way to grieve is and for how long it is supposed to last before we are over it and then try and move on with our lives. Who says that will ever even happen anyway? To be over it. To move onward and feel alive again. Will this ever happen again? What's a normal life after the death of your beloved child? Does anyone have the answer to that question? If you do, I sure would love to hear about it.

I just so desperately wanted to get away from everyone and also get away from myself. Away from all the heaviness and pain that I was feeling. I took off for a few days and went to Newport, Rhode Island, a place in which I have always found much solace. I walked along the Cliff Walk and tried to soak away my pain in many countless bubble baths. Anything to help. I felt lost, and so very much alone. I took Steven's pain medication with me. I did not think I could handle one more day of this pain and I longed to be with my son. I stood in the bathroom staring at this empty shell of myself in the mirror contemplating what to do next. I took a few pills knowing I would just go to sleep and rest, and then I got scared and made myself throw up and flushed the rest down the toilet. It gave me solace in knowing that I had more at home. They were there waiting for me, just in case I needed them when the pain got to be too much to bare.

I went to bed later that night and promised myself and I promised Steven that I could do this. I could find a way to make peace with myself and mend my broken heart. I just had to. Cody needed me and I needed him too. I knew life was going to change drastically. I just had no idea what was coming next. And yet I felt worry and fear about the future. I didn't feel any sense of anything warm or happy to come. I just felt pain. A couple days later, I was at home taking a bath. I was home alone. I left the bathroom door open and heard the door knob to Steven's room turn and it sounded like someone was opening the door to come upstairs into the hallway. My dog Kelsey started to growl and then bark. Then I heard Steven say, "What are you barking at?" in his funny, happy voice. I heard it as if he were standing right there in the hallway across from the bathroom door. I felt paralyzed, cold, and scared. I shut my eyes tight. I felt him come into the bathroom and stand outside the bathtub curtain. I am sure he felt my fear and wished he could have made it easier for me so we could be together at that moment. Shortly after, I knew he was gone. I felt so sad.

About a month after Steven passed, I knew I needed some answers, some assistance to help me make some peace with all of this and why he had to die in such a way. I felt compelled to contact a psychic medium. I looked online for one close to my area, and to no surprise whatsoever, there was none. I asked Steven to help. Soon after I found a name, it appeared as if out of nowhere. So, I immediately sent her an email. I wrote, "I lost my son to cancer a month ago, can you please help me contact him as I need some answers." I anxiously awaited her response. She wrote me a paragraph describing the incident in the hospital in which he used his hand to call to me, a time of which no one knew except for me and my friend that was there with me. She asked me to describe the details for confirmation. I did just that and she contacted me right away and set the date to come over to my house. She knew only my first name as well as my address and cell number. Before she arrived, I went into Steven's room and told him she was on her way and to please find a way to connect with her. I often heard that it is not a good idea to connect with those that have crossed over so soon as the soul was still so connected to the earth. I didn't care. I had questions that needed answers. I stood by the bulletin board hanging above his desk and looked at the pictures of his prom. Seeing all his friends smiling faces, including his prom ticket stubs. This gave my heart so much peace and happiness. I looked at the prom tickets and thought to myself, "I hope you had an amazing time at your senior prom. You never said thank you for the tickets and all that we did to help make it wonderful for you and your girlfriend so I do so hope you loved it. Did you do all the things you wanted to? Was it a happy life? Was there anything missing other than more time? Did you experience things, drugs, sex, everything a teenager does?" I never said any of this out loud; I just asked it in my mind. I also asked about what happened in the end. What took his life, etc?

When the medium arrived, she stood on my front door step and when I opened the door she said, "Are you Denise?" When I nodded she said, "Oh my God, you must have had him really young as he was a man right? A young man. He was with me in the car the whole way over. He said you have a lot of questions but first he wants to tell you that his friend that's coming over today, a name that begins with an A or an M, he said you know who she is. Please tell her not to worry about what to do with the letters that she writes to him. Please tell her I am with her when she writes. I hang out with her; we listen to our music together when she writes. She does this in her room mom; she and I made the CD together when I was sick." I smiled and said, "Yes, her name is Amanda but Steven called her Mandy. I am seeing her later. I will tell her this. It will make her so happy." Then she walked into my house and asked me not to show her around, to just stay in the living room so she could focus on what he was saying to her and not focus on all the things in the house that were connected to him. She put her hand over her heart and said, "I don't want to cry so please try very hard to control your emotions so I can connect and give you the answers he so desperately wants to share with you. I know you were devastated when he died so we'll talk afterward. During the process, I will have my eyes closed, connecting to him and it will all come through fast so I am going to talk fast, to try and get it all out before he has to go." She sat down in the corner of the room and closed her eyes before taking in a long, deep breath. I'll sum up what she said, "A grandmother figure is here, and she says she is your grandmother on your father's side, her name begins with an L... Louise? No, she says it's Lois. She said she was with you when he was crossing over, she said she felt so sorry for you in that you had to watch your son suffer so. She wished she could have been there to help you, to take away your pain and suffering. She said she is here to tell you that she loves you and she thanks you for loving her so much and she knows you just want to talk to your son so she brought him here to be with you as he has been in heaven too short of a time to have the ability to do this on his own at this point. She said yes, she was there waiting for him when he crossed over just as you knew she would be."

She went on to say that my grandmother was strong and stern and that she was not so much a religious person as she was a spiritual one and that her bible time was more of a meditation time for her to feel peace. This made sense to me and gave me comfort as I didn't want her to be disappointed with me in that I wanted Steven to come forward to be with me. As soon as he was there, the medium put her hands to her chest and said, "It's so hard to breathe, it hurts my chest, oh please take this away so I can focus on what you need to say, I am pregnant and don't want to feel so sick. Oh ok, so it was in your chest, an infection that would not heal? Yes, an infection and yes Mom, the cancer was still there, it was always there. In the end, it was the infection that my body could no longer fight." He went on to describe the hospital stay and said that he heard every single word that was spoken. He said he hated it all, he hated the chemo, it made him so sick. He was so glad when it was over. He felt relieved. He did not want to be sick anymore. He didn't want me to worry anymore. He hated that I was so devastated; he said it broke his heart. He talked about the little baby girl in the hospital and said he is taking care of her now. He said I saw her name on the white board, he told me to look at it when I was walking by it. I remember that moment very well. He then talked about the blue paint and his hands and how he tried to make me laugh but I was not having it as it was not funny to me at all. He was sad that I hurt so much when he died. He then said, "Yes mom, I loved the prom, I had a great time with all my friends and teachers. And yes, I did a lot of things that made me happy, I had sex, I did drugs, I was a normal happy guy. Nothing was missing mom, thank you for loving me so much." And before I knew it, he was gone. The medium had helped me to make peace with the end as I wanted to be sure that we did everything we could for him in his life and in the end through his illness.

After we were done, she came with me to see his room and looked at pictures, she said, "Oh my God, you were just devastated. I don't know how you were able to get through that." She saw a picture of a group of guys on the shelf. She pointed to my ex and said, "This one is so in love." I said, "He was once. He is my husband and that photograph was taken at our wedding." She looked shocked and said, "What? I would never have thought that you were married. I do not feel any other soul in this house except for you and your sons. This person is not here at all; in fact, he has not been here in a very long time." I said, "I know. He sort of checked out through the whole illness and is not doing really good right now." She said, "Well, if he wants to leave then let him leave. Why make someone stay that does not want to be here. Good riddance." I hugged her and said good-bye and thanked her for helping me get to receive some answers and confirmations for what I already knew. Funny thing is, after she left, I could not find her contact information again on the internet. The cool part is that at this time, she was new to doing this professionally. I thought it was perfect and completely unedited. She added nothing of her own thoughts until later when we were done. It was such a gift for me.

Shortly after that, my ex asked me if I was happy. And there it was, my greatest fear was playing out. I felt my heart and my stomach clutched by the hands of devastation. I responded by saying, "Am I happy? Really? You are asking me this now, just after I buried my son in the ground. Am I happy? No, I am not fucking happy, I am devastated." He simply just nodded and started to walk away. But I knew there was more he needed and wanted to say so I told him to finish what he had to say to me. He stopped walking and turned to look at me and asked me if I still loved him. I said, "I love you, of course I do, but I don't like you very much. You were not there for me or for Steven through all of this. It was hell and you just buried yourself in work and ran away like a child. So how could I really love you right now? I don't know if I will ever get that back or feel the same way about you that I once did." He once again nodded and said, "I'm not happy and I want a divorce." Everything started to spin, I felt like I was going to pass out. He walked away and left me there to deal with this once again on my own. He left and was gone for days. He refused any counseling and didn't want to tell anyone. No one knew but me.

The day he came back, he said he called his realtor friend and the house was ready to go on the market and that he wanted me to start looking for a place to live. He said that he did not want to hurt me and that this was best. So, I grabbed the nearest thing I could get my hands on and threw it at him, hitting him in the head. I was so angry that he made these decisions all on his own. He didn't give a shit about Cody or me. All of a sudden, he started to back away from me. I could see the fear in his eyes. He said, "Why are you being so confrontational, you were never like this before and why does Steven not want me here?" His face was pale. I responded by saying, "Did you honestly think Steven was just dead and buried and that he was not going to protect me and his brother? That he would let you just take away our home and walk away like nothing ever happened? He never thought you were good enough for me." And at that very moment I felt Steven standing right behind me and he said, "Not even close! Don't back down Mom, I've got you." I told him that we were not selling the house. The home that we all shared as a family. I was not having Cody leave his home nor was I ever planning on cleaning out Steven's room and moving away from where I felt his presence most of all. I told him that if he wanted to leave that he should leave but the house would belong to me. I told him I would call the bank in the morning and then contact a lawyer to start the paperwork to get a mortgage in my own name and release him from everything. He said, "Okay, but I am not leaving until it's done." As you can imagine, this took some time. It was a time in which our home was a most unpleasant place to live in together, to say the very least.

His unhappiness created a difficult home environment for both Cody and me. Thankfully, the paperwork for the new mortgage was complete and the house was all mine and not a moment too soon as I was truly at my breaking point. One night before I left to go out, he asked me where I was going. So, I turned to look at him and said, "None of your business, why do you care anyway?" So, I just left and went to meet Kevin at his office to talk. He said I should get away, go clear my head and not worry about my soon to be ex, and that all he cared about was selling the house and making his money back. He wanted to help me but I told him I needed to do this all on my own. I felt so thankful I could share this and be with someone who always made me feel better. When I got home, he was waiting for me. He asked me where I was so I told him I was with Kevin. He said, "I'm so glad you had someone to be there for you when I wasn't." I said, "Me too, I don't know how I would have made it this far without him, he is a very special part of our family and has been for many years." Then he said, "Let me ask you a question. If you could do it all over again, would you have married him instead of me?" I literally pounced in my response, "Yes! Absolutely! Without a doubt, I would have married him. He would never have left me to handle Steven's cancer and death on my own. I know he would never hurt me, no matter what life may have thrown our way." He simply just nodded and walked away. I didn't feel bad about saying this to him. It was the truth. I was so angry with the way he was treating Cody and me.

Later that night, while he was packing his things and doing his laundry, he sat down on the couch in the living room to take a break. I was in the kitchen. I heard a knocking on the door to the attic which was in the living room. I smiled as I knew it was Steven. It continued. I then heard him say, "Oh come on! Why are you doing this? Why don't you just open the door and show yourself?" I could not help but to laugh to myself as I knew he was scared and yet all I felt was Steven's love, light and protection of me. I walked into the living room and stood in the doorway. I saw the fear in his eyes with all the color drained from his face. I smiled and said, "What's wrong?" He said, "I know you heard it too Dee Dee! Why is he doing this?" I said, "He is always here. But maybe he is here now to tell you to just go and he is making sure that everything is okay." He started to cry and said, "Doesn't he know that I loved him too?" I said, "Why don't you tell him that yourself." He begged me to go downstairs to get the last of his laundry out of the dryer as he was petrified to go downstairs and walk through Steven's room to get to the other side of the basement. I said, "I am not doing this for you. You have to go make peace with him and tell him how you feel all on your own." He went downstairs for what seemed like hours, and once he came back upstairs I knew that he felt better. He said they talked and everything was okay now. I said, "Good. I'm so glad that you did this before leaving." The next day I left early for work and when Cody and I got home, we found a note on the kitchen table, it read, "To Dee Dee, Cody and Kelsey, please remember me as the person I was and not the way I am today. I'll always love you guys." And that was that. Peace… OUT!! Never to be seen again, literally.

The next day, Cody and I were making dinner and when he was setting the table, he put his plate and cup where my ex usually sat and said, "This is my chair now. I am the man of the house". At that very moment, I told him it was time we re-did the house and made it all our own. There would no longer be any empty chairs in our house. Cody and I took apart the heavy wood table, carried it outside along with the chairs, and put a *free* sign on it. We took the top off the Jeep, headed to Pier One, and bought ourselves a new kitchen set for just the two of us. That started the process of the new paint colors in every room and the new décor and the new path in life. Needless to say, the divorce came and the lawyers took care of everything so I never had to see him again. Not ever. We exchanged only one phone call before the final date to discuss some last minute legal things. I told him that I did not want him to contact us in any way ever again. I also told him that if Cody ever wanted to see or talk to him that he would do so on his own. But that day never came, there was too much pain inflicted upon us to want someone in our lives that tossed us aside so easily.

From that day on, it has been just my son and me. I don't want to focus this story on my son's journey as I truly feel that story is only for him to tell. This story focuses more so on Steven and me and our journey. But I will say this, through it all, Cody always came first, we all did our best to protect him, to keep him happy and to live the best life that we could. Cody always did amazingly well in school and in sports and had a lot of friends. He was always busy living life and I kept my pain hidden from him so he would not have to feel he needed to take care of me. I was his mother and my job was to make sure he lived an amazingly happy and fulfilled life. Life was as normal as it could be for an eight-year-old that had just lost so much in such a short time.

I believe that everything happens for a reason so for my ex to simply state that is was just too much pain for him to stay, letting him go was not that hard in the grand scheme of things yet to come. To be honest, there really is not too much more to say about him since it is so small in significance along this journey of my life. My emotions came in waves, all the anger, the grief, and the devastation gripped me in ways I feared most of all. There was no chance for getting help or counseling since he refused to do any of that. I tried everything to make it better and then the end came anyway and it was all over. Just like that. I never felt more alone in my entire life. I felt Steven with me always. I knew he was trying to tell me it was okay, to let him go and to know it would be best for me later. I don't think I was capable of getting past each day. It was all I could do but try to just survive each day as it came. I felt like I was on an island all alone, I cannot even remember anyone coming to see me, to see if I was okay. The only person I remember being there for me was Kevin. So unconditionally, he was always just a text or phone call away. He and I had been friends for over eighteen years and even though we never saw one another much as we got older, I never forgot how it felt to be around him. He was there for me now. He was the one I called when it all fell apart. I think I was in bed for four days without eating or showering. I couldn't move. Nothing I did helped me. On that last day, I had no voice left and no more strength left within me. I called him at two am, left him a voicemail message, and told him that I needed him. This was hard for me since I always took care of myself. I could barely speak so I wasn't even sure if he would know it was me. It was early morning when he called and asked if I had called and left a message as he had the phone off so there was no telephone number showing up in missed calls and he could not understand the message as the voice was so soft. I just started to cry and he said, "I'm on my way." Just a few minutes later, he walked through my door and I just fell into his arms feeling his love for me just completely surround me. He held me close and kissed my forehead. I never wanted to leave that embrace. I can still feel it today. In all my life, I have never felt that kind of love from anyone. He was so selfless, so caring and so gentle. It pained me to see the fear in his eyes showing how worried he was. He reminded me of how much I had been through in my life and that this was something that I too would get through. He said I was the strongest person he ever knew and that I had to get off the couch and get it together. He always made jokes and made me laugh except for that day. This was the first time that he showed his fear and his worry for me. I could feel his heart pounding when he hugged me. It's the way he spoke to me that I knew I could do it because he believed in me. He was my friend. The only friend that seemed to be able to handle anything that came from me. I appreciated this. Nevertheless, I also knew it was not going to be easy for me to move forward.

You see, the day before that, I had an entire bottle of pain medication in my hand standing by the kitchen sink. When I was getting a glass of water getting ready to swallow all of them, I felt someone slap my hand from underneath, and the pills went everywhere, it was then that I heard Steven's voice say, "Mom, that's not gonna change anything." I cried and said, "Steven, please, I don't know how to do this, I can't breathe, I can't get out of this black hole, please help me, please stay with me." I laid down on the floor and cried and then picked up every pill and put them away. I kept that bottle for a long time. Just to remember where I was at that point in my life.

I am most grateful for Kevin and simply just to thank him for helping me to save my own life is quite an understatement. There will never be the right kind of words to express what I felt for having had him to help me believe in myself and to live once again. He and I share a special love for each other, one that I have never experienced with anyone else. Life moves on and people have to grow and continue on their path. This was hard for me; I just wanted to stay in the warmth of those moments with him forever. But that was not meant to be. We both had our lives to live and so it is. My heart will always have a place for him. As hard as it was for me to move forward, I just knew in my heart that I had a life mission to take part in. One that was quickly unfolding right before me. And I was ready.

Chapter 6

Healing

I started medical massage school on Steven's birthday, January 5, 2004. What better way than that to start living again. I knew that this was something that had always called to me and that I had to do something to help all the children in need while they too were suffering through cancer. I knew how much those sessions at Yale put my child at rest in a deep comfort zone so I was bound and determined to do the same for others as well. After all, who better to help than someone who understood all of which that road had encompassed. I had no fear or concern in knowing that many of my healing sessions might take place in the children's hospital. I looked forward to this journey. On my very first night of class, I met a woman named Vicky. She sat in front of me. She kept turning around in her seat staring at me. I thought to myself, *What's this connection all about?* Soon after, we all started working on one another and she and I were paired up first. This was no surprise to me of course. She worked on me first and I felt an amazing connection. I knew she had gifts, much more than just being a massage therapist. When it was my turn to work on her, she quite comfortably laid on the table and let me do my thing. After we were done, she said, "Dee, do you know that you are a healer?" I said, "What do you mean?" and she said, "You are a healer. You have healing hands; a healing energy, a warm light flows through you and into your hands and into me. I can feel it." I asked her to tell me more about this as I just felt a comfort in being with her and I knew she had healing abilities of her own as I had felt them too when she was massaging me.

We made plans to get together at my house later that weekend. When she arrived, she asked me if I wanted to connect to Steven. I replied, "Of course". I was all in! So, I laid down on the massage table in the spa room that I had created in Steven's room, and we got to work. As soon as I closed my eyes and she touched me, I felt as if I was travelling out of my body and connecting to another place and time. Sort of like astral travel, only to a place that I knew was as close to heaven as I could get to from home. I immediately felt Steven come stand next to me, he took my hand in his and he stayed there with me. I could feel him. I could feel his love and his warmth. It was so beautiful and completely euphoric. I felt like I was in a dream state surrounded by soft, flowy, white curtains flowing softly all around me. I believe this is something most often referred to as *the veil*. This energy seemed to fill me and my spirit with so much love and beautiful bright, white, healing light. I felt that if I could have sat up and pulled the curtains, aka:*the veil* back, that I would actually see Steven standing right there beside me. I focused on my breathing and just tried to stay in that moment for as long as I could. I never wanted to leave this place of comfort that he shared with me. I soon felt Steven being called away and I begged him to stay. He came back for a few more minutes before letting my hand go and leaving me. After a few more moments passed, I was back in my body and brought back to the room. I slowly opened my eyes and saw Vicky standing there watching me with a soft smile on her face. I asked her what that was all about and she replied, "Dee, I took you out of your body so that you could connect to your son in heaven. He came and stayed with you holding your hand and when it was time to go, I tried to end the connection but he told me to wait, that you needed him just a little bit longer so I waited for him to tell me when it was okay. Then he left. Did you feel him Dee?" I cried and told her what took place for me. It was an amazingly beautiful connection. I wanted to stay in that light forever so from that point forward, I did everything I could to learn about all of it, the light, connecting to the other side, meditation and anything else that would bring me closer to my own spirit within so I could connect to my son and feel that love and light every day.

Weeks later, the grief started to heal a bit, enough for me to venture forward and make some new changes. I worked on changing up things in the house, again, painting the rooms, changing everything to bring in more light and a softer energy for Cody and me. Between working full time and spending the evenings with him doing homework and going to his many baseball and soccer practices and games, we tried to live a full and happy life. Yet I always felt like something was missing. I missed Steven every single day. I hung out in his room just to feel closer to him. Eventually the scent on his pillow faded away and I knew I needed to dig deeper inside myself to try and heal this huge gaping black hole in my heart.

Weeks turned into months and months turned into years. I still tried to heal the black hole in my heart. The grief still gripped me so often that I was afraid it might stay with me forever. I bought all kinds of essential oils, herbs and teas, and read a mountain high number of books. Most things I somehow seemed to know about, as if they were already part of my memory banks from another place and time. Intuitively, I knew I still had to do some much deeper work to help myself heal and to learn more about what it was I was supposed to do with my life other than have a full time boring job so I found a psychotherapist named Sharon who I knew would be a good fit for me at that time. She was giving a lecture at the Mark Twain House to a large crowd of people. I don't remember what the topic was at that time but I do remember her quite well and the essence of her. At one point in her lecture she said she was receiving a message for someone and that this was not something that she normally did. She said she worked with the angels and shared messages for all but was not so much into the mediumship side of things. I felt it was Steven sharing a message for me about learning to find the peace within for deeper meaning and for healing. She kept looking in my direction. Our eyes met a few times and I knew that this message was meant for me. After the event, she found me and said, "I think that message was for you." I said, "I know it was. Thank you so much. May I please contact you to set up a session?" She agreed and our journey to healing began. I worked with her for around ten years. All our sessions helped me seek deeper within myself. I felt supported so that I could dive into things much deeper than if I were doing it alone. It helped me moved forward. I was afraid to do it on my own as I was not sure where to even begin. And when I did let myself feel things, the pain was too deep and it left me feeling a deep, dark place of pain, grief and despair. So much so that I felt like it might swallow me whole and I would never come out of it. I guess most might say it was depression but I think it was all just part of the grief. It was something that I needed to learn to live with and to try to move forward with, without it taking over my life and making me want to quit living. Whenever I felt the grief come in, I could not stop the pain or the tears, it was so strong that it took everything else away from me. It brought me to my knees; this is something I have never experienced in my life. There is always abundant support for the families of children with cancer at the hospital, but on the day that they die, that goes away too. One is left to seek support on their own. This is not an easy path for everyone. Especially someone like me who needed something deeper, something more spiritual and not simply just talk therapy. I did not want to talk about it. I wanted help in learning to live with the loss of my son.

I started seeking healers, massage therapists, reiki practitioners, and anyone I could receive healing with to help me to feel better. This made me want to learn to practice meditation daily so I could feel lighter. It helped me a lot. I was starting to let go of the fear and had to learn to trust myself and trust that I was being guided towards something bigger than myself. I read a lot of books but none of them talked about connecting to the angels and asking for their support and guidance along the way. I thought there was no such thing as God at this time in my life because after all, how could there be a God when my son had to suffer so much before dying? Why would he ever let that happen to so such a beautiful human being? I thought I must have done something wrong to make him hate me so much as my son was gone and I was gone too. Why wasn't he helping me to feel better? Why did all of this have to happen? How would I make it through this? I started to quickly learn that being home, in my house, in our house, I felt safe. I did not want to leave the house; I wanted to be home, a place where we once all shared together as a family. I loved taking baths and lighting candles and incense and staying in my quiet sanctuary. I didn't have to be around everyone else whose life was moving forward. Everyone moved on but me. At least that was how I felt at that time.

I found an amazing healer named Hedy. She had a way about her, one that made me feel as if we may have been connected somewhere before, like in another time. A time that allowed her to take me deeper into myself to help heal that hole I had in my heart. I went to see her for readings and for healing sessions. One day when she was doing a healing on me, she played very specific pieces of music when she worked on different parts of my body. One piece in particular was so intense that I immediately felt pain in my heart. She said, "Breathe deeply through it, and let it go." I cried so hard that I wanted her to stop but she continued telling me to breathe through it, to keep pushing forward. And then the pain stopped and I cried even deeper as I felt so much love and light all around me. I felt Steven there and I could feel that he had a young girl with him. It was the same girl in the hospital. It was Laura. I wondered why they were both there together. It made me sad as I knew then that if she was here with Steven, then she must have been with him in heaven too as her spirit was so light, just like his was. I immediately thought of her mother and the pain she must be feeling as well. There was a song playing and the young girl sang so beautifully, it was a song written for her mother. It just touched my heart so deeply. When the session was finally over, I was emotionally and physically wiped out and yet I felt a huge weight had been lifted from my chest. Hedy asked me what I was feeling, and I told her about what I saw and felt. She said, "My dear, that song was written by a young girl named Laura. She wrote it for her mother before she died." I replied, "I knew it was her, I know her, Steven knew her, and they were friends. She was in the hospital with my son in September of 2002. I met her the day she was leaving to go to another hospital." She smiled. She confirmed that she had passed in the other hospital and that she knew her mother. Laura was, in fact, in heaven with my son. Now how beautiful is that? I do not believe in coincidences, what she shared with me proved it was her. She said she was told to play the song for me. It was amazing in so very many ways, and yet, she had no idea of the connection for us all prior to that session.

I do believe in exit times and I do believe that the soul does sometimes have a choice in this. There is more than one exit time for all of us and sometimes we do get to choose which way to go. However, sometimes our soul is needed in heaven sooner, and the original exit time is chosen for us. I knew Steven and I had a connection before we were both born and at this time I was still learning about what all of that meant. What was it that I was supposed to do next? What was I supposed to do with our connection to each other? I knew he was around a lot, especially when I saw clients for healing sessions. After medical massage school was over, I dove right into learning everything else. I soon became a reiki practitioner and that only magnified what I already had within me, a healing body, mind, and spirit. This was my gift. My blessing. It was my destiny, my journey, and I was ready to open that door and learn all I could to grow as a healer so that I could help other people to heal and to teach them how to heal themselves.

I went to school for acupressure, reflexology, spiritual mediumship, breathing meditation, aromatherapy, chakra healing, healing with crystals, healing with herbs and teas and tonics, angel card readings, etc. You name it, I learned it. At this time, my mother told me that my great grandmother was a healer and that she practiced massage and healing by performing cupping and using herbs and her healing hands. She said she used to do it on my grandmother for her headaches. She gave me a book on intuition and said she had it too but never wanted to learn more about it as it scared her. I took it all in. I learned and I practiced. I helped people to heal and to feel better. I was blessed enough to have the opportunity to work with those that were sick with cancer and see progress in their healing and their comfort when they were not meant to heal but to get ready to cross over into heaven. One thing was for certain, I knew I had found my journey and I was going to be open to learning everything that it encompassed. It was like remembering the gifts I surely had in another time, as it all came so easily to me. Like remembering something I knew in a past life. I just loved that.

One day I was asked to go see a little girl who was in the hospital. She had cancer and had the same doctor that Steven had. I went to see her and her parents. I stopped by the nurse's station to see if her counts were strong enough for me to be able to perform any sort of bodywork on her before I entered her room. Sadly, I was not able to as she was not well enough so I knew what I had to focus on when I got there. I walked into the room and saw her parents. They looked so hopeful and told me all about their daughter's treatment protocol and the doctor and how much they loved him. They asked me countless questions as to what Steven had and how his treatment was and I was so happy to be with them sharing their experience with them. I smiled at their daughter and she welcomed me into her room so lovingly. It was when I gently placed my right hand upon the top of her foot, looking into her eyes that I knew she would soon be going home to heaven. I felt it, I could see her there and I could smell it. To me, there is a specific scent that comes from someone when they have cancer. It's very strong and all encompassing. It takes over the sweet smell of a person's body. And yet all I could focus on was the light around her. That's the energy that I could feel the strongest. There was a beautiful bright white light within her and around her shining so brightly within her eyes. I could feel the angels all around her. I also felt Steven there with me. Holding my hand and holding hers. And I knew he would be with her when the time came. I hugged her and told her that she was beautiful and that I hoped she felt better very soon. We all visited for a while longer before saying good-bye.

The next time I saw the family was at their daughter's funeral. It was beautiful. Dr. Haagstrom, the beloved doctor of the children, was there playing music with his band for her. Now I ask you, who does this? He is an amazing person, so full of love, and support, not only for the children, but also for the parents. A true earth angel. I hugged them all once I was in the receiving line. When I walked away the dad followed me. I knew he was keeping so much buried deep inside to stay strong for his family. I hugged him and said, "It's okay to grieve. It's okay to cry and show your emotions with your family. They know you love them and are there for them. They want to do the same for you. They need you as much as you need them. If you don't, you will only bury it deeper and you won't heal in the way that I know you want to." He hugged me and thanked me while crying. I asked Steven to please come be with them and send his love so they could get through this and move forward with love and peace in their hearts.

Everyone is somehow touched when someone dies. We all have a journey to live and some are meant to be shared with those in heaven and some are not. Sometimes we have things to learn from these passing's to help us to make changes in our lives and to help others with later on. Sometimes the cause of death is so horrific that it's hard to make any sense of why it had to happen that way. For those that have lost their child to suicide, I can relate to quite well. As a mother, I experienced this with my son, not once but twice. Yes, he did not die by his own hand, but when he did take the action, that powerless feeling came over me like a tidal wave of fear. As a parent, it's up to us to love and nurture our children, to care for them and make things better in any way that we can. Right? It's our job.

When one of our children takes their own life, the kind of pain a parent is left with is incredibly intense. We wonder what we missed, what we didn't know, what we could have done to prevent it. Murder, tragic accidents, and all other types of deaths bring about all different types of emotions. It's just the way it is. I cannot tell you how many people have said to me, "At least you got to say good-bye, at least you go to see him grow up, etc." Yes, I did get to share eighteen amazing years with my son. Yes, I did get to tell him I loved him and hear him say it back. But I never got to say good-bye nor did I ever want to. Even though he was so incredibly sick, I still held onto hope. I prayed a miracle would come and he would get better. Three weeks in intense intensive care watching the life leave your child is awful. In fact, there are no words to best describe this. No one wants to see their child sick or taken from them before they have lived a full and long life. There is no such thing as a better way to go. Really, how could any one way be better than the next? Or be easier to find peace with. Loss is loss, no matter how it happened. It's the aftermath in which we are left with. It's about how we learn to deal with it that that counts. How we heal and move forward is not so easy for everyone. I know many beautiful people who never made it through this. They have either gone home to be with their children in heaven, or they wish they did and keep themselves medicated in some way.

The method of survival is different for us all. There is not one way, there is no right way, and there definitely is no wrong way. This is our life. I ask you this one question, "How do you want to live it?" If you don't know how, then take the necessary steps to start to learn more about who you are and what makes your heart and soul happy. Once you figure out what is making you feel so crappy and not wanting to live anymore, just maybe there is a way for you to mend this so that you can move forward and live your best life. I am not saying that things are mended enough to actually go away forever, what I am saying is that when you can find a way to learn to live with things and to make peace with things, to release all that no longer serves you, can sometimes really make a difference in your future. You have to at least try it right? If you don't know where to start, seek someone to help you start the journey. The path will unfold naturally once you take the first step. Trust me on this, it's true. I've been there too. You are as alone as you want to be, remember that.

Shortly after Steven's death, I was in my office when I received a phone call from my mother. She NEVER called me at the office so I immediately felt abundant fear as soon as I saw her name and number on the caller id. I hesitated before answering as I had felt Steven with me. I knew it was not going to be good news. As soon as I picked up the receiver, I heard and felt her panic, her fear and her overwhelming sense or worry. She said that my sister Kim had suffered a brain aneurysm and that we needed to get to the hospital right away. I called out to my son as soon as I got into the car. I asked him to please go be with his aunt Kim and to help her so she would not be afraid. I told him that we could not lose her now and to please do what he could to help her to stay with us.

I drove off heading to the hospital to see my sister. It seemed like hours went by before the nurse finally came out and the first thing she said was that my sister was stable and could only see one person at a time and that the visits must be short and very calm. Then she said, "She is asking to see her sister Denise." I think my brother-in-law was in shock as I know he wanted to go in first. I felt bad but I also knew why she wanted to see me. I took a deep breath before entering her room. She was so pale and had so much pain in her head. It broke my heart to see her like this. As soon as she saw me she started to cry and she said, "Dee Dee, I am so so sorry. Steven was here. He came to stay with me; he held my hand and told me not to be afraid. I saw him Dee Dee, it was so beautiful." I tried so hard to fight the tears but I could not so I hugged her and told her that I sent him to her so that she would feel better and not be afraid. She told me how much she loved me and I told her the same. Then out of the corner of my eye, I saw my nephew Jared looking at us from the doorway, as soon as I saw him, he started to cry and walked away. I knew he did this because he heard what she said and I knew how sensitive he is and hearing this must have been hard for him. You see my sister does not really believe in such things. But on this day, Steven showed her that there are angels and that he was there to help her. I know this made an impact on her life forever. It changed things for our relationship as well as I think she finally understood what I was going through. Needless to say, she recovered and is fine today. Thankfully, it was not her time to go.

I seemed to have many clients that were coming to me to help them through their fight with cancer. I knew this was a sign for me to help them in any way that I was meant to. I was always guided to use specific types of essential oils and I was guided by the angels as to what areas of their body to place my hands upon. Whenever I did this, I could feel their pain, their tumors, the areas in which they received radiation and the areas that needed loving light. So, I would ask Steven to help me and ask that he bring the angels from heaven to shine their love and light through me so they could feel better. Some healed and some were not meant to as it was their time to go home. Those sessions were incredibly beautiful for me. I never knew who was sick until they arrived, I could see it and feel it. It was only after their session that they shared with me what they were going through. Those who were open to receiving energy healing and those who knew much about it always said the same thing after they were done, "Do you know that you have healing hands and/or do you know that the angels are with you when you do healings?" Each and every time I would smile feeling the depth of their words as they touched my heart and soul. I would always respond the same way, "Yes, I do know this. It's just part of who I am and have always been. It's a beautiful gift that I have been blessed with and I truly thank you for sharing your experience with me. It means so much to me."

Shortly after my sister's aneurysm, I was laid off. I smiled to myself because I knew I needed to be doing more and that as much as I liked my job and the people I was working with, it was time for more. More money and more abundance to help me along my journey. The human resource director was a friend of mine; we had worked together years before so she had known Steven when he was young and healthy. When she was giving me this news, she put a box of tissues in front of me. When I smiled, and said that I was okay, she said, "I have only one word for you Dee… 'Resilient'. YOU ARE RESILIENT!" I carried that with me as I moved forward taking on contract positions growing and moving forward onward and upward as best as I could. As much as I knew I was meant to be doing my healing work, a mortgage still had to be paid and I had a lot to shoulder as I always had to. Being an independent person, I preferred to spend my life as a mom on my own; there was literally only a short window in time when I was with my ex that there were two people to pay the bills. Shouldering life alone always seemed to be who I was and still am today. Dating? Nah… no thanks. It was just not worth it to me. I needed to walk this path on my own and I knew it. Nothing had ever made more sense to me than to stick to the path, grow, and learn on my own. It felt empowering and so very freeing. I loved it.

One thing that helped me to feel better was having Steven's friends around. They were at my house a lot while he was growing up. I loved the way they considered me as being a special part of their lives. Some still call me Auntie Dee to this day. I have loved watching them grow up and make a good life for themselves. Some roads were not as easy for some as they were for others. But nonetheless, they each moved forward along their path in life. On Mother's Day of 2004, I was in the living room, trying to watch a movie to take away the pain I was feeling inside, as I knew so many mothers were celebrating this day with their children. Since Cody was only eight, he was busy outside playing with his friends oblivious as to what this day meant to me. I only wanted him to spend each and every day having fun so I buried my pain inside. I heard a car coming down my road; I knew the sound of that car all too well. I had heard it so many times before. The stereo blaring, the sound of the subwoofers thumping to the beat of the drums, a sound I had always looked forward to hearing when my son was pulling into our driveway. Nevertheless, on this day, it was not him coming home and that sound made me want to cry, so I got up and looked out the window, and there was Steven's car, parked outside the driveway. I opened the door to see my nephew Gary and four of Steven's closest friends (Brendan, Bill, Ian and Nick) walking up the driveway with huge smiles on their faces. My nephew carried a huge bouquet of the most incredibly beautiful wild flowers and pink roses. It was gorgeous! I have never seen another bouquet to match the beauty that this one held, not ever. I cried as soon as he hugged me, they all hugged me. Gary said that Steven wanted them to surprise me for Mother's Day in this way. It was a beautiful day and I was so very grateful. A very special moment to keep in my memory bank, that's for sure. I think of them all each and every Mother's Day and I smile.

Mother's Day - May 2004 - The "Boys" - Gary,
Brendan, Nick, Bill, Me w/Kelsey, and Ian.

On October 30, 2004, I was asleep when I heard the phone ringing in the middle of the night. I just knew it was bad news about my nephew Gary. I answered the phone, and sure enough, there was his mother on the other end of the phone line telling me that Gary had been in a very bad car accident and that the outcome did not look good. She asked me to come right away. Immediately, I called out to Steven to tell him to please help. He was already with me and he said, "It's okay Momma, I've got this." Apparently, Gary had hit a car head on and after his car was done spinning, it had wrapped itself around a telephone pole. As he did not have a seat belt on, his body was thrown around the car like a rag doll. The sunroof and part of the car's roof was pushed up by the impact of his head hitting it and the side of the car that was crushed created much of the damage to that side of his body. To see this car, one would not believe that anyone lived through this. As soon as I saw him, I noticed his jaw was pushed to the side of his face, blood coming out of his eyes, his ears and his mouth. I was devastated. I stayed with his family while he underwent surgery waiting anxiously to see how bad it was. Since there was so much damage to his head he was in a drug induced coma to help him to heal. When I saw him lying there with those tubes, I was instantly back in the hospital with my Steven during those last three weeks of his life. I shook it off and reminded myself that this was Gary and that our Angel Steven was there to help him. And at that moment, I was thankful that Steven was in heaven and could help my nephew come back to us.

They looked so much alike that it was hard to not picture my son lying there too. It took a while for him to heal. One day his mother asked me to *do that thing that I do* to help him heal. I made a blend of essential oils and put them into a bottle of baby lotion to use when I got there that night. She said she knew I could help him get better. With that love and trust, she left the room with the others and then it was just Gary and me. I had to fight to push down the fear, reminding myself that I was not alone and that the angels were with me as was my Steven. I put the lotion on my hands and rubbed them together. I held them to my heart and closed my eyes asking the angels in heaven to help me bring my nephew home again so he could heal and live a normal and happy life. I closed my eyes and put my hands on his head. I felt like we were magnets, the pain and intensity of the injury felt like a massive vibration of energy, pain, and intense throbbing through his head and into my hands. Then my hands got very warm and I felt this incredibly intense love and light all around me, and all through me and then I felt it go through my hands and into his head and his body and encompass the space all around us. I kept breathing in this abundant love and white healing light keeping my hands on his head until the throbbing stopped. I then moved my hands to his body, his arms, his legs, and his feet. Once the energy shifted and felt lighter, I kissed his forehead and told him it was going to be okay and that Steven was with him but that he was not there to take him home, he was there to help him to come back. I told him to please come back and not go with Steven to heaven that it was not his time yet. I then went to hug his mom and siblings before leaving to go home. The next day, Gary was awake and out of his coma. He had a rash all over his body but I knew it was all part of the release, not part of the healing lotion. It was necessary to bring him home again.

This healing process took a lot of time; it was very hard for his family to watch as his brain swelling caused him to be angry and violent often saying things that made no sense and things that were hurtful. One day his mother called and said I needed to come right away, she said he was talking about the accident and he was pretty upset about it. When I got there, he said, "Auntie Dee, I'm so glad you are here. Where is Steven, why hasn't he come to see me?" I had to turn away from him for a minute to compose myself before I lost my shit. I was NOT going to lose it and cry. I could not do this, not now. So, I smiled and said, "Honey, what do you remember?" He responded, "Auntie, this lady came out of nowhere, she hit my car, it was my red car, she hit me and just left me there, the fucking bitch, she didn't even stop to see if I was alive or dead, can you believe it?" It was too much for me to bear. I couldn't take it. As soon as he closed his eyes and drifted off to sleep I ran crying from the room. It broke my heart it hurt so much. His mother came to hug me. She said she was so sorry.

Needless to say, the next day was even worse. She called me at work crying telling me it was bad, and that he remembered everything, and that he was calling for me. When I got there, he was slamming his walker on the floor so angry. The nurse came in to calm him down and tried to make him get back into bed. When I walked into his room, he saw me and said, "Auntie, I am so mad. It was not my red car, it was Steven's car and I ruined it. I broke my promise to Steven and I ruined his car. I loved that car Auntie and Steven loved that car. I saw him Auntie, Steven came to sit with me on the grass until the ambulance came. He stayed with me and told me that everything was going to be okay. He was there Auntie, I saw him." I responded, "I asked him to come be with you, to help you so that you would be okay. It's just a car honey, I know how much you both loved it, but Steven would not want you to be so angry. It was an accident. It's all going to be okay now. He would not want you to feel bad about this. He is so happy that you are alive and that you are here with all of us. It's okay. Please try to let that go and heal." And he did just that. He got better, almost 100% better. The only thing that lingers is some short-term memory loss. But other than that, he is pretty much completely healed. This was one incredible miracle. We all knew that Steven was meant to be our guardian angel. Time and time again, he has shown us this gift. Even those who never believed in heaven or the angels sure had a change of heart after that day.

Chapter 7

Self Love

Have you ever felt so angry feeling that others have too often let you down in some way? Learning to have self-love for who you are truly does help to open your spirit, to open your heart and soul. It is something I often felt that I was here to do. Having been born to parents like mine, I always felt alone and later learned that I was born to my parents so that I could grow up and learn about self-love and just to be the love that I am no matter what type of challenges I might face down the road. The overflow of love is beautiful and sharing it is a gift. When you do this, your heart will overflow with that love and you will find that you are much more at peace with yourself and with the world around you. You will see others and their self-love, and you will move on from those who are not quite there yet. There is no judgment. It's quite simply just a peaceful feeling, gently moving you forward along your path in this life.

When I was seeking spiritual mentors, teachers, coaches, etc, I understood pretty quickly that every teacher has their own insights and awareness. It helps if you try just simply taking what fits with you and leave the rest. Everyone is different and some things resonate more so for others than it may for you. There is no right or wrong way. Do what feels best for you. As I was on my self-love journey to a deeper sense of healing after the death of my son, I searched for meditation centers, yoga studios; anything that I felt might bring me some inner peace and balance. It took me a long time to understand that meditation is so easy once I learned to just breathe!

Every time I put on a guided meditation CD, or played something from my long list of *massage zone* music, I could not stop all the thoughts that kept flowing in my head. It felt like I was still not connecting my body, mind and spirit yet. Even though I know that connection is always there, I still had to learn to breathe through all the thoughts that were keeping my brain from connecting deeper within.

What worked best for me is as simple as this, I stopped trying to control the thoughts in my head, I let each, and every emotion just flow through, as it needed to. The painful memories seemed to subside most days, and on the days, that it was there front and center, I asked for help from Steven and the angels so that I could process it and let it go. I was still carrying onto the fear of what could happen if I let the pain in. I was afraid that if I allowed it all in, that it might consume me like it had in the beginning. Back then, I could not stop the pain of grief and it would only manifest itself into something much bigger and much stronger than I was able to handle on my own. It would take me down, quite literally, to a state of mind in which I could not shake. It made me feel like an elephant was sitting on me. I could not move and I could not breathe. To stop that feeling from creeping back in, I found a daily ritual that really helped me connect deeper within myself and I felt better.

The very first thing I did was change up my entire bedroom. I painted the walls a warm, soft pink to signify love. I added a beautiful little chandelier to the ceiling that was controlled by a dimmer switch, which just set the mood really well. I hung soft, flowy, white curtains and added more candles to my dresser and night stands. White candles, as I felt that white signified purity and heavenly light. A beacon, if you will, to call in the angels. I bought a beautiful incense holder and a ton of frankincense, myrrh, and rose scented incense sticks. To me, those were the three blends that called to me. They reminded me of spiritual divinity and my connection to heaven. They made me feel so good when I lit them. I decorated my walls with candles, paintings of beautiful paths surrounded by trees, fireflies, fairies and angels. I bought beautiful bedding and many pillows to create a spa-like type of setting. I loved that. I had six fluffy and very inviting pillows to lounge upon whenever I hung out in my room. I bought rose quartz crystals to signify pure love and crystals that helped to magnify the energy of love, light and peace. Amethyst, citrine, celestite, clear quartz, Herkimer diamonds and angelite. I created an altar on top of my tall dresser by placing my candles, incense holder and all my crystals in a way that felt beautiful to my heart. I found beautiful music to meditate to; sometimes I listened to guided meditations to help me connect until I learned to do it on my own. I loved listening to music that made me feel loved, nurtured, and helped me to connect to my spirit. Every night, I would close the shades, light a candle or two, burn the incense, and turn on my music. I would then lie on my bed and cover myself up with my cozy blankets, place an eye pillow over my eyes and begin my deep breathing to help me get to the place I so longed to be. For me, the longer and deeper that I breathed in through my nose and out through my mouth, the faster I was able to connect within. Eventually, it got easier and I felt myself being surrounded by the angels and their love and light. I always felt Steven with me so this soon became my daily sanctuary. It was the only part of the day that I really felt connected to. Everything else just felt like a routine. Doing the things that I had to do to keep a normal balance for Cody and me. All pretty normal stuff, just not enough to completely fulfill my heart at that time. My meditation time was my saving grace. It still is today. It's also a time to connect to our loved ones in heaven. Not only do I encourage my friends to practice this, I also encourage and teach my clients that have children in heaven to meditate and ask for answers from their deceased loved ones, their children, angels, guides, and guardian angels. With daily practice, this becomes easy to do and love and light will always flow through, no matter what. This is beneficial for those who are seeking healing and connection within.

I soon started taking more classes, to learn all I could and keep my brain focused on the things that called to me. I loved aromatherapy and using essential oils so I began making my own blends and used them for myself and for my clients. They work like an accelerator magnifying the energy in the room and within the person who is using it. There is something so powerful and so beautiful that takes place when using aromatherapy. I find it quite therapeutic and healing. I made aromatherapy sprays, bath salts and sugar scrubs using different blends for different purposes, for sleep, for love, for peace, and for welcoming in the morning light. They are still part of my daily routine today.

I know that by reading all of this you may think it seems easy. I assure you, it was not always easy. I still carried a lot of pain and grief inside. This seemed to never actually fully leave me; it followed me around like a black cloud. I tried to deal with it the best way I could. I didn't know what else to do other than all the things I was already doing and practicing and still learning about. There is no time limit as to how long grief is part of daily life. To say that time heals all wounds is an understatement. Time does not stop for us to grieve. It continues onward. We either have to continue along the path or stay stuck in a place that only serves to be a vortex for the pain to gradually just increase. I knew I really needed to be ready, to be fully vested in myself before I could reach out to those I felt could help me to go deeper within. To work with angel therapists, healers, intuitives, etc, you have to be ready. You cannot force this connection to take place, as they will appear when you are ready. *When the student is ready, the teacher will appear.* So how do you know if you are ready? Trust me, you will know. Have faith in yourself and the rest will happen on its own. There is a world of teachers out there, once you open yourself up to receive more, it will flow in naturally to you.

I used to question why my son had to go home to heaven at such a young age. It took me years to learn about the soul connection one makes before being born. Remember the story I shared in the beginning of this book and my dream with Steven and I sitting on that rock in heaven? All of that made sense to me at this point along my journey. I knew I had healing gifts, blessings if you will. I also knew that I needed to understand exactly what it was that I needed to do with them. I knew Steven was special and how much he loved children and animals so I knew he was surrounded with them in heaven. He comes to me whenever I am working with a client who is not well, whether it be physically, mentally, emotionally, or spiritually. I often feel him stand behind me, wrapping his arms around me so that his hands connect through mine as soon as I touch someone. Healing love and light from heaven. This is who he is and this is what we share together as one. If I can help even just one person learn to connect deeper within themselves and create that happy space, then I know my work is done. It will always continue in this way. Steven reminds me every day to just be love. He shows me the sadness in the children, the teenagers, and in the animals. He helps them to feel love from heaven. He says that the world is a tough place for them now and how much they need our help and to be loved and nurtured. He wants everyone to feel this love within so they can live their very best life. This is our journey - this is who we are - this is what we came here for.

You too can have a greater sense of heavenly connection all the time. This connects us to our souls every day. You don't need to go to heaven to feel that when you can do it here, all the time. Focus on meditating and focus on self-love and doing all the things that make you feel alive, happy, and peaceful. As I am writing this, I can feel Steven with me, he is saying to remind you to have fun!

Chapter 8

Spiritual Connection

As much as I loved being home and working on my meditations, and my writing, I felt drawn to the ocean. There is an energy there that calls to my heart and soul whenever I spend time there. It makes me feel like I can bring my worry, my sorrows, and my fears there and toss them into the ocean. Since the power of the ocean is so magical, and so incredibly strong, I always felt that it would wash everything away and I would be renewed again. This ritual works for me, every time. I love the ocean. Walking barefoot in the sand just grounds me so deeply. I feel completely rejuvenated. There is a very special place in which I used to spend early weekend mornings at to write outside under the trees. It's called Harkness Memorial State Park in Waterford, Connecticut. Eolia was one of seven Harkness residences. The Roman Renaissance Revival-style mansion has forty-two rooms. Designed by the New York architectural firm of Lord and Hewett, the mansion was built in 1906 by William and Jesse Stillman, sister of Mary Stillman Harkness. Named Eolia after Aeolus, God of the winds in Greek mythology, the estate was purchased by Mr. & Mrs. Harkness in 1907. Architect James Gamble Rogers, known for his work at Yale University, designed the interior renovations, the pergola, and the carriage house. Rogers converted the interior of the mansion to neoclassical style. The new color palette chosen to adorn the renovated residence was in keeping with Mary Harkness's expressed desire to evoke the feeling of the inside of an oyster shell.

During the 1980's, a hurricane tore off the mansion's copper roof; consequently, Eolia was boarded up and access denied to the public. From 1993 until the completed restoration in spring 1998, the mansion was open one time annually, on Harkness Family Day. The history of this incredibly beautiful place and the ocean surrounding it always made me feel so deeply connected within myself. I used to go there with Steven when he was little to fly kites and have picnics and walk by the ocean collecting seashells and enjoying the warm sunshine. Since we are both so in love with the ocean, this was the perfect place to be to get away from the everyday routine of things. I loved to hear his laughter as his kite would always fly so much higher than mine. I can still hear his voice when he would say, "C'mon mom... you can do this too, give it some slack and just run with it like me." I love all my memories in this life and feel quite blessed that I remember every little detail since I was a child.

Located in between the mansion and the ocean are some large trees with massive tree trunks. These were the perfect place for me to sit under with my laptop so that I could write under the shade for hours. I used to go there first thing in the morning as soon as the gates were open so I could set up my spot before people arrived. One day while I was there, I was deep in meditation listening to the sound of the ocean when I heard Steven say, "Don't move mom, just open your eyes and look to your left. I brought some friends for you today." As soon as I opened my eyes I had to blink to be sure I was not seeing things. To my left, very close to me, were what appeared to be around fifty birds, at least fifty, if not more. They were all just standing there, on the ground, watching me, moving slowly and hanging out there. It was unbelievable. I have never seen anything like it. I smiled as I watched them all eventually fly away. See? This place truly is magical.

One day, when Steven was young, we spent the day there with a photographer friend of mine. I had asked him to follow us around and take some candid photos of us. I have never been a fan of the posed images as they always looked so unnatural to me. I am so thankful that I did this, as these are some of my most favorite photos of Steven and me. In fact, the front cover of this book was taken on that day. It's my most absolute favorite photo of us.

Harkness - Waterford, CT

Harkness Gardens

My favorite place to write my book - underneath the
large trees, surrounded in beautiful serenity.

Part of my journey in the writing of this book has taken many years as I needed to go through the different stages of grief and moving forward. As you can clearly see, this took years for me to accomplish. I only wrote when I felt inspired to or was called to. It hurt me too much to write about the pain of all I went through and all that Steven went through. He reminds me that it had to be this way. It had to be deep, otherwise, I would not have gotten to where I am today. I needed to be reminded of my life's journey, my healing gifts, and my ability, to do so much more than just live a normal life. He said he was sorry I had to suffer so, but that was necessary to open the door to my new path. My new life. My destiny. His destiny. Our destiny.

Steven's journey is and has always been surrounded in abundant love and beautiful light. He says to always remember that heaven is about all of us. It encompasses all faiths and religions, as there is no one that is without a heart, a soul, and a spirit. He said it is not about any particular religion or God, it's about your own soul/spirit and your journey to find out what your path in life is. For the parents who have children in heaven, he says it's about the deceased child's journey and how it's connected to yours. Sometimes it's all just part of the path and to remember that life is a gift no matter how long or how short the time here may have been. He says to never be afraid of death. His greater soul has expanded since he went home to heaven. He gets to expand out with all lovingness and he is helping teenagers cross over to the other side. He says that part of his heavenly work is to help the troubled ones. He says there is a lot of belittling and trashing going on here on earth. He is helping people be kind to themselves and to others.

One day I asked him to show me what it was like for him to cross over. I knew I could handle it at this point in my life so he wasted no time in showing me. I will say this again, "If I could paint, what a painting this would be!"

He said, "Close your eyes mom and take in a deep breath, it will be fast so hold your breath and focus." As soon as I took in a long, deep, beautiful breath, I saw a bright white light, amazingly beautiful light, it sparkled as if it were coming from a massive diamond cut with billions of facets, and it drew me in. I then noticed the *tunnel* all around me; it was dark as if all the lights had gone out. I wanted to go to the light so I felt myself being drawn into it, and then I saw a quick flash and I was back here, and the light was gone. He said that the tunnel was what he saw, he left his body and the lights went out around him for a flicker of time, and as soon as he saw that light, he went to it and it opened a doorway to the most beautiful place he had ever seen. He then told me this, "Mom, I wanted you to see what I saw but you cannot come be with me now, I showed you this in a blink of an eye so that you would understand how incredibly beautiful it was for me to leave my body and come here. I want you to know that this was my choice. I am happy here mom. I get to do things I could never even dream of doing if I was alive. You'll see mom, I'll show you more as time goes by. I love you mom. Live your best life and please laugh again and have fun like we used to always do together."

In the winter of 2007, I was not feeling quite myself. I was working full time, trying to balance my busy schedule and making my life as full and happy as humanly possible. I was also having some issues with my left foot. I had had over ten procedures over the years since I shattered my big toe joint in 1992. After seeing the doctor, I learned that the bone fusion had broken and they needed to re-do it. I knew this was going to be a crappy time as I remembered all too well, what the other surgeries felt like. Bone surgery pain is not a fun thing to recuperate from at all. The pain runs deep. Without getting into detail here, it's important to state that the surgery went well, but the swelling had caused a major issue for me after the next few days upon surgery. The long metal brace the doctor placed from below my knee to just above my toes was adhering to my skin. It was excruciating to say the least. I knew it was happening and was doing all that I could throughout the weekend until I could get to the doctor on Monday. Cody was away for the weekend with friends so I could rest. So, it was just my dog Kelsey and me. She was pretty easy and of great comfort to me. My little *nurse nana*.

That Sunday afternoon, I let her outside to do her thing and when I didn't hear her bark to come back inside I knew something was up. As she was a Jack Russell Terrier, she was notorious for getting into things. One of her favorite things to do was to roll in another animal's feces and mark herself so she could hunt and prey. A completely disgusting habit of hers, one that made me almost puke every time I had to clean her. This day was no exception. When I finally made it to the door to check on her, in horrific pain I might add, I saw her sitting on the patio just looking at me waiting to see what I would do. She was covered in black gunk. Since I could not make it outside in the state I was in, I basically had to bribe her to get her to come inside with a cookie since calling to her and yelling for her to get inside did not work. She slowly sauntered into the breezeway and when she did, I had to grab her by the collar so she would not run into the house with that gunk all over her. She smelled awful. Words cannot describe the stench of whatever it was that she had rolled in. She was covered from her back, to her neck, to the side of her face and the top of her head. I had to put my shirt over my nose and mouth to keep from vomiting. I threw my crutches down, sat on the floor, and basically dragged her inside on my bum - across the kitchen and down the hall into the bathroom. All the while she was pulling back trying to get away. When I finally got inside the bathroom, I put her in the tub and turned it on filling it with bubble bath at the same time. At this point, I was soaked in sweat as I was in so much pain. I could feel the swelling increase so intensely that I thought for sure I would bust right out of my cast. It was hell. Once she was finally clean and dry she immediately took off and went to lie in her bed. It took every ounce of strength I had left within me to get to my bedroom and change my sweat soaked clothes. I cried the whole time I was doing this; I was in so much pain. So many emotions and so much frustration took over every single molecule of my being. I screamed these words aloud, "I cannot take this life anymore. Why is every day such a struggle to survive? Why am I still in so much pain? The grieving comes in waves I cannot control. I am doing everything I can to live a good and happy life. I have beautiful people that come to me for healing and it's helping them so why can't I receive the same in return? If YOU want me to do this, to continue to help people to heal and to learn to heal themselves then show me a sign that I am on the right path. Show me a sign that more is coming for me because I don't know how much longer I can do this. Please. I need your help."

I spent the next few days searching for music to help lift my spirits. Deeper, spiritual and meditative music. I found some guided versions from Hay House that I absolutely fell in love with so I ordered more. Something told me to add myself to their mailing list so I would receive news and updates. This made me happy as literally everything that was part of Hay House always connected directly to my spirit. I fell in love with Doreen Virtue's Angel Oracle Cards, and Wayne Dyer's books and meditation CD's. Shortly after I received an email, announcing Louise Hay's new movie called *You Can Heal Your Life* and I just had to have it! I ordered it and paid for overnight shipping. I kept a close eye on the tracking so I could get home ASAP to watch it. I had no idea why this was so important to me but it called to me in a very strong way and I knew there must be something special for me about to unfold. As soon as I sat down to watch it, I was immediately drawn to the main character, the woman who was sharing her story. I was her. She was me. She spoke about herself and her life in the same way that I did. I never knew anyone else who felt that way let alone discussed it openly. It is a beautiful movie full or love, light, encouragement, realness, and filled with music that is so beautiful. I was in tears by the time it was over. At this point in time, I had felt like I had done all the work, that I had done everything humanly possible to help heal my life myself. The one thing that stood out for me was the fact that I really did not feel that the cord connecting me to my ex was completely released. I thought I had gone through all those emotions enough that is was done in every way. And then it hit me. I never told him that I forgave him or myself for everything that had transpired between us. I never said it aloud or truly felt it happen even within my own mind. I went to bed that night listening to beautiful music and asking the angels to surround me in their love and light so I could somehow make peace with all of this and move forward. So, I said it… I said it out loud, loud and strong. "I forgive you. I forgive us. I forgive myself. It's time for us to no longer be connected so we can both move on. We deserve this peace." I felt the cord cut; I felt the release of all the pain I had been carrying in my heart and soul since 2002. I felt strong and I felt free for the first time. It was an incredible gift. I felt thankful. I felt happy.

Shortly after that day, I was at work, in my office cube, or *cubby* as I like to refer to the space as; I was eating lunch at my desk and checking my emails. I rarely did this except for on the weekends as I never used it much back then as it was. I came across the following email from Hay House:

From: "Hay House" <listadmin-hayhouse@hayhouse.com>
To: Denise Willis <deewillis@netzero.com>
Date: Wed, 30 Jan 2008 16:56:33-0800
Subject: Has Author Louise Hay Changed Your Life?

Has Author Louise Hay Changed Your Life?

Have you read the book or seen the movie You Can Heal Your Life by Louise Hay? Do you feel that You Can Heal Your Life has changed your life? What changes have you made in your life since then? Do you believe that the thoughts you think and the words you speak create your experiences? Has You Can Heal Your Life changed what you believe about yourself? Do you feel like you are a new person now? Did You Can Heal Your Life help you find the love of your life? Have you changed the way you parent your children? Have you decided to start life fresh? Do you now consider yourself a positive thinker?

The Oprah Show is looking for people who have experienced a positive change in their lives after reading the book or watching the movie You Can Heal Your Life by Louise Hay.

If this sounds like you or someone you know, please email the show producer atshowinfo4tows@sbcglobal.net. Please tell us how you have used what you learned from You Can Heal Your Life and how it has worked for you in your own life. Please respond only if you would feel comfortable sharing your story as part of an upcoming show on Oprah. Please submit your story by February 1, 2008.

Hay House Inc. ~ P.O. Box 5100 Carlsbad, CA 92018-5100 ~ (800) 654-5126 To remove yourself from this mailing list, please visit this Web page: www.hayhouseimages. com/Lyris/GoodByeHayHouse.htm

When I was reading this email, I thought to myself, *How beautiful. I am so glad they are doing this. I know it will help so many people as it did for me.* I closed my email and went back to work. I felt Steven with me, his love and his warmth all around me. He said, "Mom, share your story. You're going to be on the show. It's important Mom, it's going to help so many people." I responded, "No way, I am not sharing my private, personal story like a damn Jerry Springer show. No way." I got up from my desk and walked away to take care of some things. When I got back to my office, he was there. He said, "Please Mom, this is important. Do it for me, do it for you, and do it for everyone that won't have the strength to make it through what you have." Again, I ignored it. And then my friend Donna, who was in the cube to my right came over and said, "Well?, aren't you going to listen to your son and do this already? He is just going to keep coming back till you do it." "What"? I responded, "You heard him?" She said, "Yes, he is pretty adamant to get your attention. You should listen to him." And with that, she turned and walked away. Okay. So, I guess I had better do this. I opened a new message window and quickly typed in my story. It took me all of five minutes to do this and because I did not want to change my mind, I clicked the send button before even re-reading it or proofing it for any errors. And it was off. I thought to myself, *that email was sent out from them to the whole world. Universally, everyone who had ever purchased anything from Hay House and who was part of their email list got that email, surely there are many stories meant to be shared that are much more powerful than mine. Why would they want me? Whatever happens, happens.* I let it go and moved on with my day never giving it a second thought. I could feel Steven with me. I could feel his hug and his smile as he was proud of himself. *Pain in the ass*, I thought to myself as I smiled.

This is the email that I sent to Hay House that day:

From: Denise Willis
To: showinfo4tows
Subject: Louise
Date: Thu, 31 Jan 2008 13:29:53 GMT
Good Morning....

While I certainly realize how very many emails you must have received by now discussing life changing experiences due to reading Louise's book and movie. I do hope you will read mine and not consider me just another person who wants to share their story on TV. This is not my intention at all. I have had much turmoil since my son passed away from a brutal form of cancer in 2003. Shortly after losing him, my husband unexpectedly left me stating that he felt too much pain to be with me and had to move onward with his life. He said he loved me but wanted to start his life over. Can you imagine how hard that was for me - now alone and trying to mend my shattered heart. You see words cannot describe how much pain a mother feels when she has to bury her beautiful 18-year-old son. This should have been a time for support and love and not the opposite. I was super mom; I did everything for my family and was always a very positive and happy person. I had no idea how much I was burying deep within my own soul.

Through the last four years I have tried so many things to feel better, purchased so many books, so many counselors, so much bullshit. One day I found Louise's website and kept my eye on what was to come. Only recently, I purchased her kit including the DVD, Jim Brickman CD, and beautiful daily aspirations. I watched this DVD and felt that a door that had been closed for a very long time had been opened in my heart. DEEP within my heart where I buried all the hurt. I have forgiven my ex. I have forgiven my son for his passing. I am now finally free from feeling as though I have to carry the torch in his honor every single day. He has released me so that I may find happiness within me for myself for the very first time in my life. I am blessed and I am so very deeply grateful to Louise. She is an angel sent from Heaven and I thank God for her and her life - she has helped so many people and I know she must be so proud of this. I wish her love and warmth every day. I am now sharing her DVD and my story with so many friends... They are sharing it with their friends and family too. To touch a soul and help it flourish and grow is a gift no one can give easily. To accept this into our own hearts is the true gift.

Thank you for taking the time to read my story. I'd like to help in any way that I can.

Much gratitude,
Denise M. Willis

The weekend arrived and I was off taking my son Cody to one of his games. We were rushing to get out the door but I could not leave the house as Steven was telling me to check my email. I said, "Later, I have to go." He said, "No Mom, it's important, check it right now." In my inbox was the following email from Ally from Harpo Productions:

> From: harpo.com
> To: Undisclosed-recipients:
> Subject: your email to The Oprah Winfrey Show
> Date: Sat, 2 Feb 2008 13:26:04 -0600
>
> Hi,
>
> My name is Ally -- I'm working on a possible upcoming show about Louise Hay and The Law of Attraction. I came across your email and would love to speak with you further. If possible, can you email me some basic information (age, address, phone number), as well as a picture for our files? We like to compile as much information as we can!
>
> Also, please let me know if it's possible to speak with you today and what might be a good time.
>
> Thanks so much,
> Ally

I quickly responded with all the information she had asked for. Less than fifteen minutes later, my cell phone was ringing. It was Ally. She had some more questions to ask me and before we hung up, she said they would be making a decision later that day as to who would be on the show and if they selected me and my story, they would let me know by the end of the day.

The end of the day came. I was painting my bedroom when the call came in from Oprah's producer. She said that Oprah was very touched by my story and really wanted me to share it on her show. She was so kind, warm and loving when she continued to describe to me the emotion that came over her and the others when they read it. It meant a lot to me and

I felt honored and extremely emotional, as I knew this was not going to be easy for me to do. I have never liked feeling like I was the center of attention, I preferred being behind the camera taking pictures and keeping to myself. I knew this was bigger than me and that I needed to do this for many reasons other than myself. I packed my bag and left at the crack of dawn the following morning. I had only enough time to get a few things accomplished before heading out. I gathered Steven's death certificate, my divorce papers, my photos and my music and headed out to catch my flight. The paperwork and the papers were required as well as the photos in order for them to complete the show once the taping was done. I told Cody, my mom and a couple very close friends that I was going. I needed their support in order to get there and not chicken out. I was a bundle of nerves the entire time. I tried to stay calm on the flight listening to music and reading more of Louise Hay's work. It brought me comfort so that I could stay connected to myself and the purpose for this event that was about to unfold.

Once I landed at the airport, I took my carry-on luggage and went to meet the driver who was awaiting my arrival. He was easy to spot as he had a board with my name written on it in big bold black letters. After greeting me and putting my bags into the limo, he asked me what my claim to fame was. I thought what an odd statement this was as I was not famous at all and I was just going to share a very emotionally painful story with the world and that was all. I didn't know what to say so I simply just said, "I guess you'll have to watch the show and see for yourself." He nodded and smiled and said, "I'll look forward to it."

About five minutes into the drive from the airport to Harpo Productions, I heard my cell phone ringing from within my handbag. As soon as I had it in my hand, I could see that it was my dad. I was a little shocked as it was a very rare occasion in which he ever called me. I knew it was a sign of some sort so I answered it and said, "Hi Dad, you are not going to believe where I am right now. I am literally in a limo on my way to be on the Oprah Show. They asked me to come and share my story. Can you believe it Dad?" He responded, "Wow, that's great kid, I'm so proud of you. That's pretty big news." We went on to chat for a little while before we hung up and I prepared my nerves for my arrival to the studio. It was snowing like a blizzard so I was afraid we might not make it there in time. It was crazy. Chicago snow is nothing like Connecticut snow.

As soon as I arrived, I was quickly whisked away to the salon for hair and makeup. I had no time to be nervous, as I just had to stay calm and let them do their thing. I was greeted by the nicest people and they made me feel so warm and welcome. Others came to see me to tell me what to expect and when they asked if I wanted details about the show and I said no. I told them it would be better for me to just go with the flow so I could stay calm. Once I was all made up, they took me to an area for the pre-show taping. I later learned that this was going to be used in the show once it was pieced together, as a lead in type of thing, an introduction to me and my story. They were all so nice and patient with me as I was doing my best to stay calm and answer their questions. When I started to cry, as I was not expecting some of the questions that they asked me, they said it was important for them to capture everything in order to fully share the depth of my story. I felt so bad as I watched the cameraman also need a tissue. He hugged me when it was over. So much emotion, it was like reliving things all over again. It wiped me out. When we finished the taping, I heard music and I knew that they must be taping another show and I wondered who the musician might be.

I was later taken to the Omni Suites to check into my room where I quickly unpacked and took a bath in the bath salts that I made the day before at home. I also brought candles to *call in the angels* with to help keep me calm and surrounded me in their love and endless light. This always works well for me. Every time. Once I was relaxed, I made my way to the restaurant to have something to eat, as the storm was so bad that it kept me inside and there was nowhere else to go but to stay in the hotel. When I got there, there was no one else in the restaurant other than a few of the people that worked there. I was glad for that as I felt like I had been through the wringer and just wanted to be alone with my thoughts. Shortly after the waiter took my order I noticed two men coming into the restaurant, one smiled as he walked by me. I smiled and went back to my reading my book. He sat a short distance away from me so I could see him from the side. He had his chin resting on his hand looking over at me and smiling. I thought to myself, *why does he keep looking over at me, does he know me?* Believe me when I say this, I was not in a state of mind to want to talk to anyone at all; I just wanted to dissolve myself into my book and be left alone. I didn't want to be rude so I just tried to ignore him and continue reading. I could still feel his energy, and I kept catching his eye and he mine. I thought, *what is this all about? Seriously, if he knows me than why doesn't he just come say hello already?* Then I heard Steven laugh and he said, "No Mom, HE thinks you should know HIM." And he laughed again. What the hell? I had no idea what he was talking about nor did I care. I just wanted to be left alone.

A few minutes later, another one of the Oprah Show guests came into the restaurant with her mom. They came and sat with me. She noticed the two men sitting at that table nearby and she said, "I know him, he is on my show sometimes. I think his name is Doctor Drake." *Ding ding ding* rang the bell in my head! I said, "Doctor Noah Drake from General Hospital?" She responded, "Yes." I laughed in response and said, "That's Rick Springfield. He is a musician. He sings that song Jessie's Girl and it came out way before you were even born so you may not know it. He was a pretty big hit back then with the ladies. My mom absolutely loved him. I remember her watching the show with my sister when I was a kid." As soon as I said that to them, they both went over to get his autograph. I knew my mother would be upset that I didn't do the same for her as she loved him so much but I am not the star struck type of person nor did I feel comfortable doing that. I think he wondered why I stayed behind because I could see the question in his eyes when he looked over at me again. I simply just nodded and got up to leave the restaurant. Why tell you all about this you may be asking yourself. I just wanted to share the story of my time there and to also share with you my connection to my son and his ever-ending reminders for me to pay attention to things. I am hoping that you will learn from this for yourself and receive your own messages from those you love and not be as stubborn as I am and ignore them too.

Later that night, I joined the rest of the people that were part of the show and we all went to a theater to watch Louise Hay's *You Can Heal Your Life* movie on the big screen. It was wonderful. I met so many great people that night and each one of us were there to honor and celebrate Louise and her beautiful movie. When I got back to my hotel later on, I took another bath, put on my pajamas, and went to bed, praying that I could rest well and not be nervous for the taping of the actual show in the morning. As soon as I closed my eyes to focus on my deep breathing meditation, a soft scent of roses filled the air and surrounded me in its splendor. I felt my son there, standing at the foot of the bed. I said, "Roses for me? Nice touch. What color are they?" He responded, "Pink roses of course, nothing but the best for you Mom. I love you. Thank you for doing this for me. Don't worry; I'll be with you the whole time. We'll do this together. You and me, just the way it will always be." The scent grew stronger as it gently put me to sleep. I felt incredibly warm, peaceful and very comforted. When I awoke in the morning, I was excited. I felt so much peace come over me and I knew I could do this. I knew he was there with me and nothing felt better than that.

When I got to the studio, I was waiting for hair and makeup and they were running behind due to the blizzard going on outside so they forgot me in the room. Someone had to come find me and walk me to the stage. But I had to wait, as Oprah was there ready to go on as well. I walked with her and she smiled and welcomed me. That helped me to stay focused on what was to come next. I felt happy and ready to share my story. Since I still had on my air cast, I had to be careful getting to my place so they seated me in the front row. Immediately that unnerved me. I tried to stay focused on my breathing and doing everything I could to stay calm. The guest speakers arrived next. Cheryl Richardson, Martha Beck, and Louise Hay took their seats on stage directly in front of me. I loved being there, being so close to these very special ladies. Oprah was on their right leading the conversation off as the show began. Behind them was a huge screen. On this screen, they were showing some of the taping that we had done the day before along with some of the photos that all of us brought to the show. When I saw myself and my beautiful son Steven on that screen, I could not breathe. I knew I was going to lose it so I asked him to please help me stay strong so that I could speak eloquently and not waiver.

Steven was right there with me and he said, "Its okay Mom, I am here with you, I will help you through this, just breathe." And so, we did this thing together, my son and me and the words just flowed. The show took over an hour to tape and I felt the energy in the studio that day, an energy of so many people, all equally as touched by Oprah, Louise, Martha, and Cheryl as I was. I had no idea how it would be aired or when or which photos they would use and which parts of the taping would stay and which would not be used. Louise was so kind and loving, after I told her the impact that her movie had on me and why, she said, "You have no idea what's in store for you. The most wonderful adventures are coming." Of these words, I shall never forget. Not ever.

The show aired on June 24, 2008. It was called *The Law of Attraction*. I told a friend about it ahead of time as I had a funny feeling that I may not be able to see it. She told me that she would tape it for me. Just before 4pm, I set up the machine to record it; this was prior to having a DVR with my cable, so it had to be done *old school* style. At 3:55pm, every single TV in my house went black. The screens simply turned black. I could not change the channels or do anything else. I don't know why I was not meant to see the show but I knew there was some reason for it. I waited it out. At 4:55pm, the TV's all came back on as the show was ending. Nice. Completely weird. My phone rang, it was my mother. She and her husband were very upset as they didn't know the depth of my pain and suffering. I tried to tell them that few could understand it at that time and that this show was to help others to heal and to offer support for them along their own journey. I told her that I was fine now and that I needed to go through my own time of grief and to not worry for me now. She said my sister Kim was so upset and was on her way over. I know it sounds mean when I say this, but honestly, where were they when I needed them back then? No one could handle it back then, why come now after hearing me share my story on national TV. It rather pissed me off. I was not doing this for attention, I was doing it to help people, but then again, I understood that not everyone would understand, and I didn't really expect them to.

When my sister arrived, I knew she felt worried, and upset, and I tried my best to remind her that I was okay, and what it was like for me, and how no one could have helped me but me. It took some time but I knew she heard me and understood the best that she could. The phone rang non-stop after that. I just let it go to voicemail after a while as it was just too much for me to handle not having seen the show yet, I had no idea what actually was aired. Most understood and a some didn't. The ones who didn't, are not in touch with their spirit, they don't know what I am talking about when I say that we have to *go deep*, and connect within, in order to heal ourselves. It's all okay to me as I get it. I understand what it feels like to be in their shoes too. All I ever wanted was to be respected and not judged by the way I felt about life and death. Nor did I want to be treated with any sort of pity. This is my life, and this is my story. It is my hope, that everyone who watched the show that day, felt something stir within them making them want to seek more, to create a better life of their own. Something to help them to connect deeper within to help them to heal their own pain and suffering just like I did and many others have done as well. I hope it helped in ways that I have yet to fully learn about myself. I hope that those that watched this show and didn't know of Louise and Hay House, have found her work, and all those that share their love and light through Hay House, are forever changed by the gifts shared from Hay House. There is something for everyone there. To me, Louise, is the beacon of light that has forever changed my entire world. I remember her words and what she wrote in the very first page of her book, *You Can Heal Your Life*: "In the infinity of life where I am, all is perfect, whole, and complete, and yet life is ever changing. There is no beginning and no end, only a constant cycling and recycling of substance and experiences. Life is never stuck, static, or stale, for each moment is ever new and fresh. I am one with the very Power that created me, and this Power has given me the power to create my own circumstances. I rejoice in the knowledge that I have the power of my own mind to use in any way I choose. Every moment of life is a new beginning point as we move from the old. This moment is a new point of beginning for me right here and now. All is well in my world."

After the Oprah Show aired, I knew what I needed to do, in order to stay true to my life's mission. My path, my journey, my mission, and everything else all quite easily fell into place. I continued doing business analyst, technical writing, and training work, and after each contract ended, others appeared. Sometimes they took a little time in between to arrive which always left me feeling stressed and worried until I chose to focus upon my faith, and having trust, that I would always be provided for. I continued to see clients on the weekends and sometimes at night in between Cody's many practices and games. My plate was full, and yet, I had this yearning for wanting more. I always felt like something was missing. The only thing that helped to ease that feeling was for me to stay busy and focused on my healing work, and on my healing gifts. I was on a constant mission to learn more, to experience more, and to stay open to all that came into my world. I had a lot of dreams in which I received lessons, and information to help guide me along the way. Sometimes my dreams were just peaceful dreams in which I spent that time with Steven, just hanging out and talking, just like we did when he was alive. The only difference was that I could not touch him.

This eventually eased for me as having him so close, and so very near to me, brought me a different kind of comfort. I could feel him, I could hear him, and sometimes, he would do things that would allow me to see, and feel, even more. He used to leave me dimes. He said they were nice and shiny and silver, just the way I liked things to be. He said pennies didn't sparkle like the dimes always did. They would appear at the most appropriate of times, just when I needed a little reminder to get out of my head and get back to myself. Always, the radio would play a song that he and I loved; this still happens today, quite often I might add. It's one of my favorite things to experience. Music and memories. Nothing better! Sometimes there were dreams that came as reminders for me to do something or they were there to help me to help another person. They were most intense during the twilight hours of my sleep but as time went onward, they started coming to me at all times. I think that is because I had finally gotten to a place where they could reach me at all times and I never second-guessed them any longer. Insights, intuitions, and knowingness appear to me when I am called upon to do my life's work. As these stories would take up an entire book of their own, so I'll just share a couple of them with you for now.

One day I was visiting a friend's house for dinner and I was *told* to look out the window. I saw a fox anxiously pacing back and forth. My friend, who had no idea that I had this *gift,* asked me what was wrong, and wanted to know what I was looking at. I told her that something was wrong with the fox in their backyard. We all went outside to explore the situation. As soon as I saw the fox, I knew it was a mother and that her babies were in harm's way. I asked for assistance from the angels to show me where they were. I didn't say anything to anyone; I simply just walked over to the area where they were stuck. They were stuck in an old well. It was half covered with dirt, and half covered with the lid of the well. I just moved the lid over to the side. Once I did that, the babies became visible. My friend's husband came over when I told them that I found baby foxes in the hole. We put on garden gloves and took them carefully out of the hole, one by one, checking them out to be sure that they were all unharmed. The whole time the mother was watching us as she nervously paced back and forth. I talked to her to try and soothe her while we got her babies to safety. As soon they were all out of the hole, they ran off to their mother and she checked them all out to be sure they were okay before turning around to look at us as if to say *thank you* before they all ran off. Once we went back inside to finish dinner, my friend gave me this sideways look and asked how I knew that something was wrong outside. I just told her I saw the fox in the window pacing back and forth. Nothing else needed to be said. I knew she would not understand if I had told her the truth.

On another occasion, it was a very cold day. It felt like the coldest winter ever. It was a Sunday morning and the sun was already out but I wanted to stay under the covers and dream. I felt Steven poke me in the arm and he said, "Momma, wake up. Go outside. I have a present for you in the backyard. It's your favorite." I got out of bed, threw on my boots and a jacket, and took Kelsey outside with me. She ran right over to the side fence wagging her tail and turning to look at me and then back at the ground near the fence. In the ground, next to this fence, were three rosebushes that never took. I had planted them the year before, anxiously waiting for them to finally bloom, but they never did so I cut them down to the ground. In the center bush of twigs, there was one, tiny, bright pink rose bud. It had about a half inch, of bright green stem on it, connecting it to the rest of the dead branch/twig. Its scent was intoxicating. It was so beautiful. I ran back into the house, grabbed a pair of scissors so I could cut it, and put it in my small rose bud vase. It was a perfect gift.

Another day, I was hanging out by my pool listening to Steven's mix of music when I heard that I needed to call my friend Vanessa. *Shit,* I said aloud. It was not a good feeling. In my mind, I asked the angels if what I was feeling was true. Did she have cancer? I knew by what I felt next that she needed a friend who understood what she was going through. Someone who could handle it, and support her, no matter what she was meant to face next. She and I had become friends after we worked together on a project. I loved her. I thought she was such a sweetheart. Ironically, she called me the next day to see if we could get together at my house for lunch. Of course, I agreed, and immediately called our friend Jackie to join us. She said she had something to share with us. I didn't say a word about it to anyone. I wanted Vanessa to share whatever she wanted to with us, no matter what it was going to be. And there it was. She told us she had cancer and that it was bad. Jackie cried and later asked me if I knew. I could only nod my head *yes*.

I was thankful to have some moments with her that were fun and some days a lot of pain and turmoil were shared, along with some beautiful moments of the three of us just being there to just hug each other. Shortly before Vanessa went home to heaven, we had a long talk. I pray it brought her comfort so she could go and not leave with any more pain or worry in her life. I knew she was ready to go. As hard as it was, it was equally as beautiful as she had fought so hard to survive that the end was very peaceful for her. I thanked her for coming to me after she died to confirm some things that took place. It made me happy and brought me much comfort. I cherished the angel wings she gave to me. She said they reminded her of me. She was a beautiful person. I know she is shining that light of hers in heaven now. Watching over her boys and all those that she loves.

Shortly after that, another very special friend of mine went home to heaven. I had met Ana while working on a project as well. I loved her from the very first moment that we met. I knew she was fighting breast cancer and I knew that she had good and bad days. She was the first woman I ever knew who simply just exuded love and compassion for everyone. I don't think she had a mean bone in her entire body. She and I got to know each other pretty quickly, and shortly after that, she would ask me to do my healing work with her. It helped her to feel better, to not have so much pain all the time. I would have done anything to help her feel better. I would go see her in the hospital and just stay with her and talk with her, hold her hand and work on her, all the while asking the angels to surround her in their love and light. I prayed for a miracle for her, as I knew how much she didn't want to leave her family. We had many long talks and many moments of shared tears. The week before she passed, she came over to take part in a workshop I was hosting at my house. I knew the time was near. I sat on the chaise lounge with her and she put her head on my chest and just cried. I asked the angels to please send all the love that they could so that she would feel it, and not feel such sadness and pain. I felt her body become calmer, and she closed her eyes, and fell asleep. We sat there for a long time, just the two of us. It was beautiful. I saw her in my dream shortly after that. She was so happy, and she told me she loved it there, and that she and her father were having so much fun. I felt her hug and kiss me before she left. It made my heart so happy. Angel Ana, this is who she is. A beautiful angel.

On December 13, 2012, I got home from work and was not feeling like myself. I knew something awful was coming only I couldn't see what it was as it was not being revealed quite yet. I lit candles and felt like I needed to ask heaven to send many angels to help. I was up all night. I just could not shake that feeling of fear, pain and worry. I felt devastated, and I knew it was going to be something big. Steven came to me that night and he said, "Mom, you have to finish your book soon, there are going to be many people like you who need help. The kind of help that comes from someone who has been in their shoes. I want you to remember this when you are writing. I love you Mom. I am right here with you." OMG. I knew by the way he said this to me that whatever was coming, I needed to continue to send love and healing light towards the pain, towards the worry and towards the fear. I asked the angels to do the same. When I woke up the next day and was getting ready for work, I still felt worry and devastation but I also felt a lot of abundant love and light surrounding me, surrounding everything. I prayed for faith that whatever was coming would be surrounded in heaven's embrace. I kept asking and praying for that. I sat at my computer and could not focus. I felt it coming much closer now. Around 9:45am one of my co-workers was so upset. He had just heard on the news that there was a shooting at an elementary school in Newtown, Connecticut. It was just too much to comprehend. I had to walk away. I went to the ladies' room and cried. I cried for all the pain that these parents would be facing once this all unfolded. I cried for the children that were not going to see adulthood, and I cried for whoever the shooter was as surely, *he* was not well, as no one in their right mind could ever harm so many innocent children. At that time, I had no idea as to what the details were. I only knew the numbers were large. Steven was with me. He hugged me and said, "Momma, please don't cry, the children are here in heaven. It was so quick Mom that the angels were already with them before they crossed over, there was no pain and suffering. They were already on their way home. Send love to the parents Mom, they need it now. You know what to do, just be the love that you are and don't stop till you know it's done." From the bathroom stall, I did just that. I sent love and I sent healing light to everyone there that day. I asked the angels to please keep doing the same. Steven showed me a small glimpse of all the children, the beautiful children, the newest angels in heaven. Beautiful little angels as well as all the others that joined them there on that day.

That night, the phone rang and I knew it was my mom. I knew she must have felt me and I also knew that she knew what I was feeling. I could barely get the words out to even say hello when I answered the phone. She said, "Dee Dee, what's wrong? Is it those children? Are you crying for them? I responded, "Mom, I am so sorry, I just cannot talk about it. I knew about it the night before, Steven showed me. The pain is just too much for me to talk about. It's like my own pain mirrored times a million. I'm sorry Mom. I just cannot talk about it." She replied with abundant anger in her voice, "What kind of a sick...." I immediately interrupted her and said, "No Mom, please stop. He was not well. It's very sad for all of them. For him, his family, and all the lives that he took today. Please just ask for love and light to surround the families now, not words of hate or words of anger. Please Mom. It's important." I told her I had to go and would speak with her later and I hung up the phone. For those of you who don't know about this day, I would like to share the details with you so that you can understand the depth of the grief I was experiencing at that time:

The Sandy Hook Elementary School shooting occurred on December 14, 2012, between 9:34 and 9:40am, in Newtown, Connecticut, when twenty-year-old Adam Lanza fatally shot twenty children between six and seven years old, as well as six adult staff members. Prior to driving to the school, Lanza shot and killed his mother at their Newtown home. As first responders arrived at the scene, Lanza committed suicide by shooting himself in the head.

My Steven reminded me on that day of his own journey in heaven. He wanted me to know how much he loved being there to help the children by showing them around and helping them to understand where they were. He said it was his greatest gift. To be an angel that gets to help children and welcome them home to heaven. I'm very proud of my son and even more proud that he chose to be my son and that we shared life together while he was alive and well all the beautiful moments that we've shared together after he went home to heaven. As for today, words cannot adequately express the love and gratitude that I feel for him and for all that he does for me and everyone else that we know and love, not to mention all the others that he helps from where he is today.

Readings, Stories, and Confirmations

The following section includes letters written to Steven; stories about him, and some of the readings that I have received from others throughout the years. There are also some very beautiful words shared with love honoring my Steven and his very special life.

Justine's Story

(My mother and Steven's grandmother)

"The first thing I remembered about hearing of Steven's illness is when my daughter called to tell me that Steven was sick with cancer. I did not believe her - I thought she was exaggerating and that they did not have all the tests back yet - I felt helpless, there was nothing I could do. I was devastated.

He was 17 at the time - when I called him to check on him he said he was angry that he was going to die and he just wanted to be a kid and live his life. So, I told him, you are alive today. Live for today. It broke my heart. It just never seemed real to me - I just could not believe that he was sick. And then the day came that I visited him in the hospital and noticed all the kids on the wall and I said look all these kids Dee Dee - and my daughter said: 'Mom, those are all the kids that died.' It was at that moment that I knew his picture would be there too one day.

He was a wonderful human being - he would sit and have an intelligent conversation with me every time I was with him - he was a joy, he was a blessed young man. It wasn't fair, I felt hopeless that I could not do anything to help him or to help my daughter feel better.

The last 3 weeks of his life, while he was in the induced coma, I touched his soft, sweet skin talking to him about the time we swung on the hammock on my patio and it broke - the two of us laughed so hard. We had so much fun together. I showed him what seaweed was. We built sand castles together. I told him of all the times that we shared. I still could not believe that he was going. I prayed to God to have him take him and not let him suffer any longer, no more treatments, no more needles, no more pain, no more suffering for my daughter. My oldest daughter Kim called to tell me that he had passed and a calm came over me and I went back to sleep. I could not reach my daughter; it seemed as if days passed. I felt lost. His death touched everyone so deeply in our family because he was so special - his death was felt by everyone. To this day, I cannot say his name without feeling the pain of his loss. To talk to my daughter and see and feel her pain and her struggle trying to heal though the loss of her son. I felt lost, so much pain that I could just not help her. This stayed with me for months. I went to counseling for weeks to talk about what I was feeling to someone that would listen. It did not take away the pain but it did help to talk to someone. The loss of a child to a grandmother will never go away - you accept it and you go on but there is always an empty chair and it will always be there- always part of me - but another part of me still feels very angry - he should be here, he would be almost 31 now, married, with a family, but that was not God's plan. This young boy changed people's lives with his illness and his passing for the better.

As his grandmother, I will go on and I will get to be with him again, but the pain in my heart will always be there. But my daughter, suffered so horribly watching her son leave her forever, leaving her to move forward on this earth. The joy she has brought to people, her healing work, helping others and just the way she lives her life, I am so proud of her, I could never have done what she has done to go on with her life. When people ask me how many grandchildren I have I always say 6, one is with God. His pictures are hung up all over my makeup table, he is with me every day when I am "putting on my face" - he is always there with me, these pictures have always hung there, around my table. Steven is here now, I just heard him say that "It's ok Gramma, you are done now." I told him it is not ok, it is never ok. The only peace I have is knowing that he is not suffering anymore and that my daughter is making her dreams come true and that she is happy. I think that is what any mother wants for her child. I am very blessed that I have the relationship that I had with Steven, and that I have all the wonderful memories of the good times and not just the painful times. I am so thankful that I have those memories."

August 2003 - Gramma (Justine) and Steven
enjoying their dance together.

Justine's most favorite photo of Steven and Me. I was
teaching Steven how to make a wish for the first time.

Ashley's Story

"Steven was the love of my life. I was 14 years old when we first met; I remember those big blue eyes like it was yesterday. The minute I met him, I knew we had a connection. We spent almost every day together; walking the school halls holding hands, exchanging love letters, hugs and kisses in the hallways, hanging out after school, etc. You name it and we were there together. I couldn't wait for class to be over just to see his face and that smile again. Our relationship was more than I could have ever dreamed of. I felt like we truly connected in a way that most people searched their whole lives to find, we even planned our whole lives out together.

Steven was a romantic, a very thoughtful guy at heart. Anywhere from buying me flowers, singing me a song or one day having a limo pick me up to bring me to Hubbard Park for a picnic. One of my favorite memories was the day he asked me to his junior prom. That was one of the most exciting days of my life. I don't think I've ever jumped so high. There were many days that we would just laugh for hours, I really felt like he was not only my boyfriend but my best friend. Little did I know that about six months into our relationship, life would throw not only him, but us a curveball.

After a fun filled summer of pool parties, Pig Roasts at Andrea and Scott's, and spending time with friends and family, things started to change a little bit. Steven loved to work out, play football and go for hikes. He loved the outdoors and constantly stayed active; however, the things he was used to doing became harder. First it started with shortness of breath, which after seeing his pediatrician was thought to be asthma. The inhaler didn't help as other symptoms started to occur. At one point, I remember him calling me to tell me the doctor's thought he had hepatitis. Hepatitis at 16, there must be something else.

After some more time passed, he found a lump. The doctors' prognosis: Cancer. Non-Hopkins lymphoma. I couldn't believe my ears when Steven sat me down to tell me. How could such a young, healthy guy get cancer? After hugging and crying for almost an hour, he said, "I understand if you want to leave", I couldn't bare it. I love this man and I could never leave his side. In my mind, I was basically married so for better or for worse.

So, the process to healing starts, first round of chemotherapy treatment here we come. We were so optimistic that he was going to beat this. Even though he was sick some days, we were constantly laughing (typical Steven cracking jokes) trying to make the best out of this situation. Other days he was upset, stressed out or vomiting from the treatment. Chemotherapy round completed, all of our confidence was high. The Connecticut Children's Medical Center and their team of doctors and nurses were amazing. The cancer seemed to be gone. We were so overjoyed. Now he can get back to building up his strength to play football and be with his family and friends.

Unfortunately, luck was not on our side or his as the cancer came back. Things were a little harder than the first time, here were go round two. More surgeries to biopsy different lumps, platelet treatments, long days of running different tests. Things weren't as funny anymore; we were growing up fast through this whole process. We still went to different events but his strength wasn't there. He would get winded easier and have to sit down sooner than before. He became outraged some days, tired of being sick and becoming a little mean even. I knew he didn't mean it but it was tough at times; especially when the person you love is going through this and there is nothing that you can do to fix it.

I tried to be encouraging; telling him he made it through once, you will make it again. Some days he really believed in getting better, some days I think he already knew what the outcome really was going to be. Yet, he kept trying to stay as positive as he could. I don't know if it was for him or just to help us through. There were days that he tried to leave the hospital just to get away from it all. He didn't want to do the chemotherapy anymore, he felt like maybe he should just end his life now. There were times that he tried to hurt himself when he was home. I did whatever I could, I cried and pleaded for him to stop, and I couldn't bear to lose him. I tried to call 911but he would lock me in a room and unplug the phone so I couldn't. There were days in between visits where I could see the healing of previous cuts on his wrist. Between the medications and the process, itself, this really took a toll on him.

Round two completed, he was in remission. Life went back to normal for a little while. He was missing his hair, had multiple scars and felt weak but he still managed to get the strength to go to senior prom. This time he wore a tuxedo, bandana, hat, and even his *pimp cane* to complete the look. This prom was a little tougher than his other one, but he danced as much as he could and kept on smiling. It was a great night and we couldn't have been happier.

Final devastation, the cancer came back and this time it was in full force. I'll never forget where I was or the look on his face when he had to tell me the news again. I told him not to worry; the chemo is going to get rid of it this time for good. It worked before, it'll work again, and we just have to stay positive. There's no way at eighteen years old he would be gone. We just have to keep trying.

Steven had it, there was no more trying. He said, "No Ashley, I'm so drained. I can't do this anymore, I am mentally and physically exhausted and I can't take anymore". I still didn't believe it, you have to keep fighting. One last time we were at my house and he tried to commit suicide. There was blood everywhere, I was shaking so bad when I made that 911 phone call. He told me how sorry he was but I knew things were bad. He went straight to the hospital and we were not allowed to see each other anymore.

Steven and I tried everything we could to stay in contact. We went from sneaking phone calls, trying to have our friends three-way call, having a neighborhood kid exchange letters for us, hiding in the back seat of his car to running away. Nothing was going to stop us from seeing each other. However, things got worse. Steven was hospitalized and we had no contact.

Weeks later, I received the worse phone call ever. I dropped to my knees in hysterics, I couldn't breathe. Steven was gone. I couldn't believe this was actually happening. Is this real or am I having a bad dream?

That was it; there were no more phone calls, letters, or possible visits. He was gone. All I had left was a voicemail on my cell phone that I kept playing over and over just to hear his voice again. Every car I heard with a sound system in it made my heart jump. I couldn't eat because I felt sick to my stomach and if I tried, I would get sick. It was like my heart had literally been ripped out of my stomach. Cancer had won.

I wondered every day if he was okay. I was sad and angry. How could God take him away from me? I re-read his letters, listened to that voicemail and looked at all of the pictures I had. One day, the strangest thing happened. I turned on the radio and our song was playing. I hadn't heard it in months that is how I knew he was safe. I could finally sleep, at least for tonight.

It took me years to cope with the pain. I tried dating different guys but no matter what they were never Steven. I constantly compared everyone to him. I went out with my friends and tried to keep myself distracted but I always found myself thinking about him. I became so depressed and nothing could fill that hole in my heart. Until one night, God came to me through a friend. He knew what I had gone through, sat and listened to me as I wept. He showed me that as painful as things had been, Steven left because he was so special that he needed to help others. My heart felt whole again and I truly felt that Steven was there with us.

Fast forward to the year 2012. I was still struggling with dating, comparing other guys to Steven. Sure, there were times where I thought I might have been in love but it was nowhere near what Steven and I had, until I met Josh. Josh was a friend of Steven's. We knew each other for years. In fact, there were several occasions where Steve and I would go over just to hang out with him. When we first got together to catch up, I felt something different, something I hadn't felt in a very long time. I had an instant attraction and connection to him, but this time it was different. In some ways, he even reminded me of him. Little did I know two years later we would be married.

Josh and I frequently talk about Steven and how we think that he had a huge part in how we're together. There have been times that we could even feel that he was with us from a warm touch as we were hugging to turning the razor on when Josh went to the store just to play a prank.

He would always find ways to let us know that he was with us. Looking back over the years, Josh and I would constantly run into each other but were always at different places in our lives. Never did either one of us think that we would wind up together, but Steven was showing us little by little that he was getting ready for his master plan. He helped bring true love into my life again I couldn't have picked a better man for myself. He is wonderful, funny, charming and loves me immensely. Although I miss Steven every day, I know that he is doing better things. I know that if I never met him or shared those experiences, I wouldn't be who I am or where I am today."

While I was adding Ashley's story to the book along with adding in her favorite photos, the wind chimes were playing as if a strong wind came by. Where I live, this never happens. At the same time, Steven was with me reminding me to add *his blessing* for Ashley and Josh. He said, "Please don't forget to tell her how much I love her and Josh, and yes, it was me who brought them together. They finally *heard* me!" His happiness in regard to Ashley and Josh is hard to miss. I am over the moon, that they are so in love, and are so happy together, as Josh is one of those friends of Steven's that made in impact on me. I always knew how special Josh is, just like my Steven is and just like Ashley is.

Ashley and Steven - May 2003 - Senior Prom

Ashley and Josh

Mandy's Story

The following is a story written by Steven's very dear friend Amanda *Mandy* Pintarich. She wrote this for Steven on December 19, 2007.

Forever Remembered

"Kate was getting ready for work at the farm. She was already running late looking for her Lewis Farms Staff shirt. Then her phone rang, it must be my boss she thought. She hastily looked down at her caller ID: Steven's House it read. But it wasn't work it was Steve, "Hey Hun!" she replied. "Hey" replied Steve not quite sounding like himself. "What's up?"

"Oh, not too much… I have cancer."

Kate's heart stopped. Wait, did she hear him right or was she not fully paying attention.

"Steve, what did you just say?"

"Kate, I have cancer, Hodgkin's Lymphoma to be correct," Steve slowly repeated.

Kate sat down, her world in a total spiral. How could this be? Steve is only 17 years old, her best friend, no, this cannot be. Only old people get cancer. Not high school football players. The phone was silent for a minute.

"Are you there?"

"Yes", Kate replied unsure of what else to say.

"So, what are you doing? Are we still going to the movies tonight?"

"Umm, well, I'm getting ready for work about to walk out the door. I'm actually running late and should have been there at 3. Yea, I'm still up for the movies. Are you? Are you sure you want to go to the movies? Are you okay Steve? What does this mean you have cancer?

"Whoa. Slow down. Everything will be okay. You finish getting ready for work, and come over when you're out. Bye Katie, I love you. Don't worry!"

Click. That was the shortest and longest phone conversation between Steve and Kate. Kate was in a total daze at work, trying to comprehend what she had just heard. This cannot be. Something must be wrong, a mistake. Steve is just joking around, I'll get him tonight. What a little shit. Kate tried to convince herself this was all a sick joke. Inside her heart was melting.

Those three hours at work were a complete blur looking back. Kate left work, stopped at home, changed her clothes, and grabbed a sweatshirt - off to Steve's. Her heart was racing. She was driving much faster than she should have around those curves in the road.

"That was fast," Steve yelled out from the back patio. Kate could tell he was trying to make her laugh; he always said she drove way too fast. That's why Steve always drove when they went places.

Kate ran into his arms, she has always felt so safe and loved in his arms. They just stood there embracing one another, silently comforting one another.

"Hey, don't look so sad Katie. I'm okay. Really. I am. So, what's the game plan for tonight?" They sat on the back patio both avoiding the obvious. Small talk between the both of them seemed so complicated tonight, not wanting to say anything that would upset the other. Both went inside to talk with Steve's mom and grab a quick drink before they were leaving to see a movie. Kate went downstairs to Steve's room to put her stuff down, everything seemed surreal. How could this be happening? Once she walked back upstairs, Kate and Steve went into his Acura Integra and drove off.

"Sweet Lady" came on over the system, both Steve and Kate smiled. Steve singing the lyrics to Kate taking her hand in his while they drove. "I hope you aren't going to be like this all night, or I'll drop you off." Steve joked around trying to make Kate smile. "Sorry, I'm okay. Let's just have some fun tonight. I'm sure it won't be that hard." Steve and Kate went to the movies to see what was playing. Nothing seemed to spark their interest. Plan B, make a few phone calls and visit some people's houses that were always open for visitors. Steve and Kate stopped at his aunt's house.

"Hello, how are you two doing tonight?" asked Steve's aunt. "What would you two like to drink, grab what you want in the fridge." Although they were both underage they grabbed Jack Daniels Twisted Punch. Both needed something to calm their feelings. They hung out with his Aunt for a few, talking about the hot summer they were having and made plans to come over tomorrow and go swimming. "Let's get going." Kate suggested and off they went to see what else their night might entail.

Steve wanted to go down Queen Street to check out all of the local high school hangouts, including the Wendy's parking lot. After all, Steve did have a nice car with a loud system to show off, complete with undercarriage lights-any high schooler's dream car. Kate and Steve stopped at Wendy's to talk to some friends. Shawn was having a party at his house later on that night. That was an option, but Kate could tell Steve wasn't exactly in the partying mood that night. "Maybe we will stop by," said Kate. But both she and Steve knew they were just saying that to be nice. After hanging out at Wendy's for a few, Steve wanted to drive some more. He always liked to drive when he had a lot on his mind.

Kate sat next to Steve, looking through his vast selection of CDs ranging from N'Sync to DMX. Kate always had to laugh seeing both in the same CD case. She chose a random mix for the next CD of choice to listen to, a more relaxing combination of music - a CD they had both listened to together several times before. Kate and Steve sat in silence for a few miles just listening to the gear shifting of the car and the changes in lyrics from one song to the next. "Want to just go back to the house, watch a movie, and relax?"

"Sure Hun, whatever you would like." Kate reached for Steve's hand gave it a little squeeze and rested her head on his shoulder for the remainder of the ride home.

"Shh...Kelsey, it's just Katie, don't bark!" Downstairs they went to relax. For some reason, Steve's room looked different tonight, Kate stood next to his bed looking around at all of his collections. She stopped and picked up a frame of Steve and his little brother Cody. They both looked so happy and carefree. "Want a drink?" asked Steve. "Sure." Steve led Katie into the other side of the basement to the old-fashioned refrigerator. "Sublime or Skyy?" "Skyy please."

Both sat on Steve's bed looking through a roll of pictures from the summer. Kate sat crisscrossed next to Steve waiting for the right moment to talk. They put on the

"Fast and the Furious", both as a way to distract one another from their day and to mask their conversations from Steve's parents sleeping in the bedroom upstairs. "Let's get some popcorn to eat." Upstairs they made some popcorn, BEEP! went the microwave when it was done. Steve's mom came out of the bedroom, "Hello Katie, how are you tonight?" "Good," Kate replied a little unsure of how to react there in her pajama bottoms and Steve's shirt. After getting a glass of ice water, they both returned down to his room. It was halfway through the movie when they had both fallen asleep. Kate woke up, started to lower the volume of the movie. "Steve, hey wake up. Turn off the movie." Steve woke up and turned off the movie. They were just laying in the darkness with the dim light coming off the lamp located at the bottom of the stairs.

Kate looked into Steve's eyes, she couldn't wait anymore. "Steve, what does this mean?"

"I was waiting to see how long it would take you. I don't know what this means Katie. This is all new to me too. All I know is that I will be starting treatment next week up at Hartford." Steve took Kate into his arms; she rested her head on his chest. Lying next to him listening to his heartbeat while he was playing with strands of her hair, she felt so safe and secure. She loved this feeling of protection and love.

"Katie, don't cry. I love you. It will be okay. Trust me. Hey, stop and look at me." With a shift of her body she looked deep into his eyes, and with that look she knew everything would be okay. "I love you too."

They would go through this together. That night, they both slept in each other's arms. Both searching the comfort of each other knowing that the next few months would be the hardest either of them would face. Kate woke up earlier than Steve that morning. He has always looked so peaceful when he slept. Kate woke Steve up with a kiss on the forehead, "It's time to wake up Hun."

"Good Morning, how did you sleep?"

"Good and you?"

"Excellent, you were here."

Steve and Kate got up, got dressed, and went off to begin their day. Both had to go to their different jobs. "I'll call you when I get out of work, bye Steve." Off they went to finish their day.

The summer was now winding down to an end. Kate was getting ready for her freshman year of college, starting a new chapter in her life. Steve was receiving chemotherapy at the Connecticut Children's Medical Center. This was an emotional experience for both of them.

"Hello Denise, is Steven home?"

"Hi Katie, Yes he is but he is sleeping right now. He just got home from the hospital. You can come over if you would like."

"Sure, I'll be over in a few, just making sure he wasn't at the hospital."

Denise and Kate sat at the kitchen table drinking tea and talking about her plans for the fall. Steve slowly walked up from his room, smiling to see Kate and his mom sitting down chatting.

Steve and Kate went into the living room to watch a movie. Steve was always tired after chemotherapy. They both just watched the movie lying together on the couch. Kate touched the tender skin on Steve's head; he had lost all of his hair from the chemo. Whenever they would go out in public he would wear a white bandana, but Steve didn't feel like he had to hide his cancer from Kate. He felt completely comfortable around her. They both trusted each other, and never felt as if they needed to hide anything.

"School is starting soon - I don't want to leave you Steve. I'll be home every weekend to see you and we can hang out like normal."

"Kate, you have to go to school. Don't worry, I will be fine. I'm always a phone call away. I should be able to drive in a few months when my chemo is over. Then I can visit you up at school."

"Okay, it's a deal. But I still don't want to go. Steve I..." Steve pulled Kate into his arms.

"Love you".

"I love you Katie, always have, always will."

The next week was move in week. Off to school for Kate. A weekend of unpacking, settling in, and freshman orientation. She was exhausted from her busy weekend. Her phone rang at 8:30 Sunday morning, Kate scrambled for her phone still half asleep. Her called ID said, Steven's House.

"Good Morning Hun."

"Katie, it's Denise, Steven's Mom"

Kate froze; her heart was beating out of control. She sat straight up in her bed.

"Steven passed away early this morning. I'm so sorry to tell you this over the phone but I wanted to tell you before you heard it from anyone else."

Death ends a life, not a relationship."

This is actually a story that Mandy wrote to share with her class. Therefore, not everything is in line with the real story of Steven and Mandy's relationship. Of this I can tell you, she was a wonderful friend to my son, she is the same way with my son Cody and me. We are still very close to this day. I remember the night they were at my house watching a movie and the other times she came over to see him with his friends. It was short lived that summer as Steven was very sick during that time. He spent more time in the ICU than he did at home. I feel blessed that he had so many wonderful friends to share his life with. It makes my heart happy. Recently, Mandy gave birth to a baby girl. She was born on Steven's birthday. She arrived into the world quite early and when I told Steven this, he responded, "Don't worry Momma, I've got her. I am watching over her and her mom and dad." I could feel the happiness and pride in his voice when he spoke so softly to me. My angel baby taking care of his best friend's little angel baby. A wonderful gift of love, that's for sure.

Steven and Mandy - May 2003 - Senior Prom

Angel Reading with Kate Massaro - January 8, 2009

Angel of God, my guardian dear
To whom God's love commits here
Ever this day be at my side
To light and guard
To rule and guide

Kate's Question to the Angels:

"Dearest angels, what message does Dee's son Steven have for me?"

"Why dearest, you have now reached a higher level of angel wisdom! Steven has let you enter a realm we did not yet know you were ready to receive. We are so overjoyed that you are 'here'. We cannot stress enough to Dee that she is resonating at a high rate, and should slow her breathing down at this time, either with meditation or laughing. Yes, we said laughing! She too needs to see her inner child awaken. Steven plays with her inner child often to keep her 'up to date' so that when Dee is open to the world of child-like innocence, she will absorb all the wisdom an inner child has to give. We are so hopeful for Dee's book, and know it will be bigger than the Eckhart Tolle book which has started the world's new awakening,

The Archangels are lined up and ready to go everywhere instantaneously!! We know Dee has no worries with her son by her side and knows she will be his twin soul in the White Realm of Wisdom we call the infinity of Information Galaxy – a fancy name that Steven laughs at all the time! "It's just Wisdom, Dude" is what Steven just said. We are so overjoyed to have Steven's molecular structure you call DNA, changed to assist us even more in getting people awakened and aware, for Mother Earth is watching and she has a plan of world peace non other has seen in any lifetimes. A world where people live in true harmony spiritually – spirits actually coming together as one in a universal consciousness we have never seen the likeness of. Purity, Love, and Decency will rule the Earth, and all that has polluted her core will be released to a black hole of consciousness we humans will never see again – this is all in the Worlds of One and One world plan for all plan. You see, Dearest, this message is meant for you and for the world, and Dee is helping spread the message with her son on a conscious level only a few are aware of right now, but when her book is released, you will help spread this worldly wisdom on a subconscious level with her and her son Steven. You and Dee are soldiers of Grace and Wisdom, and Steven is actually helping make it happen at a faster rate, for he cannot wait to be with his Mother on a new level of consciousness when the shift happens."

Kate's question to the Angels: "Dearest Angels, will you be functioning on a different level as well?"

"Yes, dearest, we will, and this will give us so much more power to help all lost souls who are getting polluted by the closed level of consciousness as we like to call it. We are so blessed to know you and your soldiers (Dee and many more to come)!!

Your life and the lives of those around you are going to change drastically for the better. You will bathe in the water of pure love and tranquility, and when your time here on Earth is done, you will jettison to levels of consciousness no other human from Earth has come close to. Dee, and others have already shown you the way, and yes dearest, this message is for you, but Steven wants you to send it to Dee, for she too will receive information from it, if she isn't already."

Thank you, Angels.
Thank you, Steven.

Kate Massaro is an earth angel. From the very first moment that I met her, I loved her, and her beautiful, kind, and very loving spirit.
To learn more about Kate, please visit: https://katemass.com

The day I received Kate's Message, Steven told me to go outside and look for my present. I brought my camera with the hope of capturing something special. I sure did! It was absolute divine timing!

Event with Roland M. Comtois

My dear friend Karn invited me to an event in October of 2009 to see a very special spiritual medium named Roland. I was nervous about attending as I have always felt so much energy while being in a room full of people that so desperately want to connect to their loved ones. Being an intuitive and spiritual medium myself, I could hear, see, feel, and sense all the loved ones that were there visiting from heaven as well as feel the attendees calling to them. On that day, traffic was pretty bad so I arrived literally two minutes before they were about to close the doors and begin. The only seat available was in the front row. It was the aisle seat and I was grateful for that space as it meant I would be able to have no one sitting to the left of me. I needed some space around me to help me stay grounded. I asked Steven to come through if he wanted to because at that time I was going through some major changes in my grief and healing and I needed some insight as to what I was supposed to do next. I was questioning my journey and wondering how long I would have my son be so close to me. I knew we had a journey to live together and share things together with, but I was looking for some confirmation.

As soon as I sat down Karn smiled and said she was so glad that I was able to make it and that I was just going to love Roland as he was such a special light and such a warm and loving person. As soon as he walked into the room, I felt exactly what she had conveyed to me. Immediately I relaxed and asked my angels and guides to help me to just breathe in love and light and to not take on all the energy of the people in the room. I felt wrapped in love and I felt my son with me, standing to my left, his arm draped around my shoulder. In my purse was one of the last photos ever taken of him, I felt inspired to bring it that night as it was different than the one I had always kept in my wallet. I soon learned that Roland wrote messages on large purple paper days prior to his events with the messages he received for those attending. I listened to him share his beautiful messages with so many people in the room that night. He was so kind and so eloquent when he spoke with such warmth and love. It was an incredibly beautiful experience. When he was looking my way, he held up the purple papers. Not one, but two messages came for me. I knew they were for me because I heard Steven say, "See Mom, I told you I would have a gift for you tonight." They read: "Did you bring my last picture?" and "Thanks Mom for taking such good care of me. I'm not sick anymore!" It took all that I had to hold back the tears of emotion that I was feeling. I wanted to hug this sweetheart of a man who shared such beautiful messages from my son.

When the event was over, I went to see Roland to thank him and to tell him how profoundly beautiful the experience was. He was so kind. He asked me if I knew about my connection to my son and how we were meant to share life together in many ways and that he was my guardian angel and that he would always be with me as we had work to do together as one. I knew this of course, but to have a stranger confirm it with me was incredible. I hugged him and thanked him for sharing this with me. He inscribed a message in my book so that I would always remember what I came here for. It reads, "Denise - His light is your light; His breath is your breath - His heart is yours. May you always know that he is Spirit.

10/6/09. "I am so thankful for that experience. I look forward to attending another one of his events soon.

For more information about Roland, and his events, please visit: <u>www. rolandcomtois.net</u>

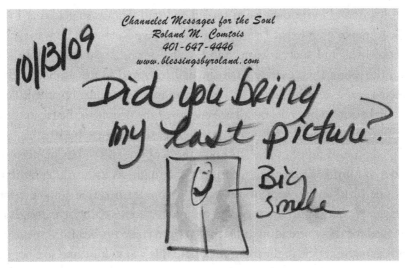

Purple Paper - a message just for me from Steven. I did bring a special photo of him that day.

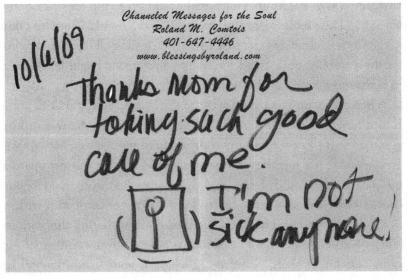

I loved this message even though it made me cry - it was most profound.

Spirit Reading by Angelic Light (Catherine Robson) - 7th and 8th June 2011

It's important for me to state at this time that although I have a very strong connection to heaven and to the angels and guides and of course, my son, I too, just like you, need support and confirmation. I sometimes question what I see, think and feel as I am a human being and I need to be sure that what I am hearing is right on target. Sometimes I just need to hear it again and again. The following is a reading I received via email from a beautiful earth angel. She lives in the UK so she has never met me or anyone else that I know. She also only knew my special/private email address that does not have my name in it so I can assure you this message is directly from my son Steven. I purchased the reading online only stating that I wanted a reading with my son in heaven. I told her my first name and his first name only. It made me cry when I read it. It's shared in exactly the way he speaks and while I was reading it, I felt him with me saying the words out loud to me. This reading is being shared in its entirety and has not been edited in any way.

"Hi Denise, Steven is here for you. He says, "Hello Mom, as you know, I have never left your side recently, for you have needed my help and assistance. You are doing well, even though you think you aren't. You will get through this time, Mom, I know you will. You just have to trust and have faith that all will be well. I trust you Mom and I know you will make the book a huge success. We will do this together, you and me and we will get our message across to the masses. There is no one better to write my book than you. I am a perfect guide for you and you are the perfect writer. We are a good team. Know that I will help you every step of the way and through your frustrations, this will help you grow in character and bring us closer."

"Remember and laugh, for through joy comes great delight and much healing. You may feel that there is not a lot to laugh about, but I can assure you that there is and when we laugh together, we can heal many things in our lives. Even though I am 'over here' and you are there, there is nothing stopping us being together. The veil is thin and it is much like a curtain, which can be drawn back any time we both have some free time. As you know, I do much teaching on the other side and this does take up a lot of my time, but you know that I will be with you in an instant when you require my full presence, so do not be afraid to call on me. I am always with you in some form, whether that be in part of my essence or in my full glory. I am with my brother also, for we have a special bond that will never be broken."

"Do not worry about me for I am fine and in good health. I do get concerned for you though, for you can be up one minute and down the next and this worries me a little in case it is putting a strain on your heart. The next time you feel so down, call on your friends and let them know. I know you do not like to be a burden on anyone as you like to be the strong one who is always helping others, but you need help sometimes too Mom and it is ok to ask for help. You will find that your friends will rally around for a few days and this will give you the strength to carry on for longer. You deserve this time to be pampered, so don't worry about asking for help – put a message on your page about how you are feeling and you will be amazed at the response. I am sure that those who get comfort from you daily will only be too happy to offer you some back in your time of need. Just because I died a while back, people seem to think that you are ok now and you put on a good front, don't you Mom? You need to let people know that you have days where you feel like ending things and they will help you. You do not have to be ashamed of this. It is a natural part of the grieving process. Of course, you would never come with me early, for you have too much to do down there and you would never give in. You just think that you might sometimes. I would never let you anyway, for you are where you are meant to be and we can work together to bring much change to humanity and of course our dear Mother Earth herself."

"Your book will be a life changer for many. It will enable them to realize how life is short, but in that time much can be achieved and many new ideas can be brought forth that will change people's lives. Do not be afraid of putting this book out there and having it published, for it will indeed inspire many to make the most of what they have and to follow their dreams. Life is too short to sit twiddling our thumbs. We need to get out there and make a change in the world if we want things to be in tiptop shape. People need to make the first move if they want to achieve their goals. The spirit world cannot do it all for them but we can help with inspiring them and guiding them to the right people and places that will assist them on their paths. Life is for living and not for dwelling on the past all the time. Look to the future and make plans and this will help you to move along quicker. Your dreams will come true Mom. You just need to step out of this pit that you are in. Once you do this, you will feel a lot better. Lately it seems as through things have been spiraling out of control for you. There are things going on inside your head that you don't like and you wonder where these thoughts come from. They are fears from your own mind, but you do not need to listen to them. Just acknowledge them and let them go whenever they pop into your head. Know they are there but release them and bring in some new happy thoughts instead. I am happy so you have no need to be unhappy. We have gone through a lot together and we will go through so much more together. This is what we have chosen for ourselves and it has made us both stronger individuals."

"I still wear my hat a lot, for it is a part of me. I went through a stage of not wearing it for it reminded me too much of the hair loss. But now I wear it with pride and I am proud of the cancer, for it has brought me here and made me who I am today. I want you to be proud too Mom. Please don't think of it as a loss or 'hate it' in any way, shape or form, for it has brought so much joy to me and it has shaped me. It is a gift in a way, although you might find this hard to believe. There is always a higher purpose at work when one gets cancer. It can be a hidden blessing for it changes things that were not right and it brings feelings and emotions to the surface that needed to be brought forth for cleansing. It also strengthens families and helps them to bond. For their love in uniting forms a great barrier of love that no one else can penetrate. Yes, there is pain but from this pain and sorrow come great light, strength and resilience. Much bravery comes forth and this is not a bad thing. We all have to go through trials and tribulations in our daily life. We all have something that happens to bring us strength or to bring us closer to our neighbors. Each person has their own path to live and each person touches the lives of others in many ways. We are all here to live our truth and spread our light so know that I done just what I was meant to when I was alive. I didn't need to stay on Earth as a physical human in order to do my work. I had done what I could and then I moved on. Now I can finish my work from here, although it is not to be finished as it will be ongoing and I will be doing this work forever. I want to inspire people to live their dreams and not to waste a single minute of their lives, for there is so much joy to be had in doing what you love. If you are sitting with a gift, use it and do not let it go to waste. Do not let your dreams pass you by. Dreams are there for the taking and the making. Use your gifts wisely and go for it, for there is nothing to lose. Never worry about what people may think of you, for that is their problem. As long as you are happy doing what you do and it brings you great pleasure and satisfaction, then that is all you need. As long as you are using your gifts with honesty and integrity then you can't go wrong. Never worry about what others may think of what you are doing. Do your job to the best of your abilities. If they like it, great. If they don't, then that's ok, for we all like different things and we all have our own beliefs. We will not always like the same things as other people but it does not mean that the creator of these things is wrong or that there is anything wrong with what they have produced. As long as they have been happy and joyful in its production then that is the main thing. Always follow your dreams and always follow the path you are guided to, for that is what will bring you joy."

"I am sorry for anything that I put you through. It was not my intention to bring you grief and pain. We had agreed on a soul level that I would pass away early for this has happened before in many lives and indeed you have done the same thing with me before where you left me early and I was left to cope as a broken-hearted father. Yes, for you were my daughter. So, I know the pain you are feeling right now and how it tears at your heart and you're very being. It is not something to take lightly or that people can say get over. You never get over it. Even to this day and even although I am in spirit, I still feel etheric pain for that time when you left me. I am always working on healing it of course and I have learned many lessons from it. But it is something that never goes away completely, for it always serves as a reminder to make the most of each day you have and be grateful for everything you have in life. Life is too short to be worrying about minor details or needless worrying about material items. Life is for living and it is for having fun! There are many lessons to be learnt on our great Mother Earth. These are to be patient with whatever life throws at you for on a subconscious level you have brought these lessons upon yourself to grow in spirit. Not everything you receive in life is your fault but you do manifest (and everyone does) things into your life to test yourself. This is all part of being in a human body. We all go through grief, despair and many turbulent times during our earthly lives. This is not the only reason we are here though. We are here to experience God's beauty and his glory and to have fun and enjoy our existence. However, for each good thing in our lives, there is always something to balance it out, such as grief. For every person who incarnates, someone dies. In heaven, when someone leaves to incarnate, a soul is brought back home. It is all about balance and it is all one big cycle. Things are always changing and things are always in motion. Time never stands still. It is always moving and changing. Much like the ebb and flow of the waves."

"Have you seen me standing at the bottom of the garden waving to you, my dear Mom? I have done this many times for I know you like to see me out there, enjoying the fresh air and having fun. I do still spend a lot of time in the garden, for it is a place that I loved when I was growing up. Indeed, I have been in a lot of gardens and I have enjoyed each and every one. I loved going to the park also. I love being outdoors."

"I will help you Mom. I will help you get through this pain, fear and anger. I know exactly what you are going through. When you come back home to me in many years to come, we will hug and we will laugh at what we have put ourselves through. But we will have grown so much and our spirits will be strengthened because of what we have achieved. We will be proud of each other. I feel guilty that I have put my family through this pain. It is not a nice feeling. But when I bring myself back to my true self, I know the bigger picture and I can see why I had to leave.

I did not mean to cause pain. Leaving was a lesson for me and it was to teach others about humility, grief and pain, so that they could be strengthened in their love and in their existence. Live life fully and never give up on your dreams. That is my message to you Mom. I want you to get out there and have fun. Spread your light and help as many people as you can. You deserve to be abundant in all ways and if you do your work, it will help you as well as bring in the abundance you so need in your life. What you give out comes back to you in many ways. Be grateful for all that you have, for you have much more than a lot of people do. Use your light to help others out of their pain and misery. When you do this, it will help you step out of your own pain and misery and it will give you a sense of purpose in life. Do your counseling, for that is what will help you the most. You understand what others are going through and this is what will keep you going through the hard times. Go to the beach and let the energy of the waves wash over you, cleansing and renewing every part of your being. Go forth, my lovely Mom and be who you were sent here to be. Although you will always carry the pain of my death, things will get easier for you and in the next 10 years, your pain will have lessened considerably. With each year, the pain dies until there is only a memory of the pain. This memory stays but it is better to focus on the memory of the good times we shared, rather than the memory of the pain. Of course, you cannot rush the grieving process, for this has to be experienced in order to get through it. You do not have to relive what happened to me though. Use what we have both gone through to write your book. Write about the pain and what you have done to overcome it. This will help others who are grieving and they will know that they are not alone, for they have others who are going through or who have gone through the same thing. Some people who are grieving feel they are going mad, but they are not. By reading your book, they will know this and they will realize that it is all just part of the grieving process. Many doctors do not have time to give or offer advice on grief counseling. They are happy just to give pills and tablets. This is not enough. Everyone who needs it should receive grief counseling. If this is done, there will be less need for tablets and less diseases later on in life, for as you know, unresolved grief can cause pain in the body that leads to physical illness if the grief is not dealt with. Part of your job as a grief counselor is to help with this. It is a very important job to have, for it is very healing and it can heal emotions before they turn into physical symptoms. What better job to have than this. If the doctors would refer all grieving people who cannot cope with their grief alone to counselors it would make their job much easier. But of course, funding cannot always stretch that far. There are a lot more counselors required in the world and indeed, if everyone could train in counseling then they could be their own counselors and there would be less need for doctors, except for medical emergencies, rather than illnesses caused by emotions. It makes much more sense to me that doctors be trained as counselors and that each person's session with a doctor should be longer than the current time. People are rushed through doctor's surgeries far too quickly and just given medication to numb their pain, instead of getting to the root of what is causing this pain. Much better to go to the source of the pain and heal it from there instead of masking it. Many people cannot talk about their emotions and this is eating them up inside. Your job in getting people to talk about their problems is very important and it is one that we encourage here in spirit. I will be with you every step of the way, Mom and I will help you with your career, for it is so very important. In my next life, I wish to be a holistic doctor and I know that you will be there in some form, helping, encouraging and inspiring me to do my very best, just like I am here to do the same for you right now."

I feel that Steven and I are twin flames. The connection we had was so special and so deep; I felt it before he was born. Twin flames are, overall, the most intense energy connection one can have. Each one of us has a twin soul, or twin flame, another whose energy vibrates on the same level or frequency and who we recognize instantly upon meeting. Not necessarily, a romantic interest, although it can be. Twin flame energy goes far and beyond the definitions of any level. It is more than romantic love, or love for a friend, for a brother or sister, for a parent or mentor. It includes all of these kinds of love, and is equally far beyond such a connection. The instantaneous recognition is because the energy one senses is actually your own. You and your twin flame were one energy in a past life. Therefore, in order to help the spiritual evolution of life you split into two so that you could learn twice as fast. There is something incredibly special about twin flame energy. Due to the nature of the shared energy, of two individuals on the exact same frequency/wavelength working in tandem, any energy work you and your twin flame do is amplified beyond that which you can do yourself. The work you do together becomes much greater this way. In the past, we have worked apart from our twin flame in order to accomplish and experience more, but as we come closer to the transition point, to the next step in humanity's spiritual evolution, more and more twin flames are being drawn together in order to bring humanity to an energetic tipping point. As for me, not only do I have this with Steven, I also know I have this with another on a romantic level. As far back as I can remember I have felt that his energy resides in California. I feel this energy when I am exploring the Hollywood hills. I believe he went through a lot to get to this point too - awaiting my arrival - it has been a very long time in coming, for both of us. Words cannot adequately express the way I feel about this. All I can say at this point is that I look forward to the connection.

Spirit Reading by Angelic Light (Catherine Robson) - 16th March 2012

"Steven is here for you today. He says "Hi Mom, it's been a while since we spoke like this through a medium. I miss talking to you like this. I feel free when I am allowed to do this, as it strengthens my connection with you and with earth more. It makes me feel happy when someone can hear me talking. I get frustrated when I travel around visiting everyone and they can't hear me. I don't like to do anything to make people hear me as I don't want to scare them. I love everyone so much and I would just love it if they would all listen to me. It isn't hard to hear me. They just need to concentrate and focus and they will hear me clearly. I think a lot of people want to hear me, but when they try they don't believe I am actually talking to them, for it is so simple that they think they are just imagining it. They think they are going to actually hear my voice and my accent, but of course they aren't, unless I do the mediumship another way, a more physical way. I love chatting. You know me. I like to talk and babble all day long (he is laughing). My wish to be a teacher would have been great as I could have talked all day long, to my heart's content. I know I drove you mad sometimes Mom, but you know I had your best interests at heart and you just gave me so much inspiration that I couldn't help it."

"You and I go back a long way, Mom. We have been together in many lifetimes. We were together in Egypt, Atlantis, Brazil, Mexico, Venezuela, the Andes, Greece and many more places that are beautiful and inspiring. We have done a lot together, you and me. This is why our love is so deep. We have been together in many different reunions, in many partnerships. We have been brother and sister, husband and wife, twins, Grandparent to Grandchild, you name it, we have done it. We will be together again and we will have many more lifetimes where we can explore our relationships. I am really looking forward to this. For now, you are my Mom and I love you so much. You are my world and you are always in my heart. I love you so much that it hurts when we can't be together physically any more, but know that I am always with you in spirit and we are still together, only on a different level. I cannot wait until the day when we are reunited and that love we share will feel whole once more. You know yourself that you can feel a hole deep in your heart, where I am not with you. This will be filled and the love will radiate out from you on all levels. You will feel whole and complete once more. Know that the angels will sing on us for our reunion and it will be a wonderful, joyful time! You know in your heart of hearts Mom that it will be a wonderful occasion. At the moment, we do meet in spirit when you sleep and we hug, but when you are truly free from your body, it will be a complete reunion and the stars will be shining bright that night. It is amazing just to think of it and for me; it will be one of my deepest wishes come true."

"Even when I was in your belly, you felt the connection between us; so, strong and so pure. You knew that when I was born, it would be incredible and it was. It was a very happy time I had on earth with you and my wonderful family. We had such good times that I will always treasure. I know that I am dwelling too much on the past, but I cannot help it, for it was just so amazing for me. Now I am in a better place and it is wonderful here, but I do miss you being around all the time. I often can't wait until you go to sleep at night so that you can come and visit me here. I know I am a mommy's boy and I am not afraid to show it (he is laughing). My friends used to tease me because I spoke about you so much, but I couldn't help having such a wonderful mom that I adored. I am always so grateful for everything you have done for me, and I can never thank you enough."

"What I went through in my last days is irrelevant to me now. It is only a whisper in the wind. All I think about now is the love we shared and the love and fun I had with my family. I do not focus on the past pains and hurts at all and I see my passing over as a blessing. I do not feel bad about it. I am over it now and I am a new person; one who is healthy and strong, with no fears. When I was dying, I was very fearful. Not of passing over, but of leaving you all. It was a hard time for me, but that has gone now, so please do not focus on it. See me as me. See me running down the beach with my arms wide open and a huge smile on my face. For that is me; not my illness. The illness was only a temporary gift to teach me many things and as a passage to the afterlife. See it as a blessing, for it brought me many gifts and surprises and it touched the hearts of many of my family and friends, who I hold dear to this day. I will never forget how kind people were to me on my last days. It was heartbreaking to say goodbye and to have everyone say goodbye to me. It empowered me though and when I look back on it; it was such a huge thing in my life to experience. It certainly had the wow factor. I want you to move on from this now, Mom, for although you say you have, you clearly haven't. I am not that person anymore. I do not have the cancer anymore. You do not need to focus on it anymore. I am me; just like I was when I was a young innocent boy. Think of me as a youngster when I had no cares in the world. I was carefree, happy, and content and loved by all of my family. I had hobbies, toys and everything I wanted. This was the perfect life. Focus on that. See me as 8 years old, when I was whole and complete and happy. That was my best time and this is what I want you to remember. Remember when I used to touch the worms in the garden or when I used to get up to mischief? Remember me like that, for it will make you laugh. I do not want you to remember any pain. Yes, it is there, but it can be released in an instant. You do not need to focus on it. Let it go to the wind, where it belongs. It does not mean that you need to forget what happened to me, but just that you do not need to focus on it. It has gone and it has happened and I am me and I am here. I love you Mom, with all of my heart, and as I hold your hands right now, I am sending you the greatest love of all."

I am asking Steven about the book you are writing together and he says "never mind the book, Mom. It will be ready when it's ready. There is no rush and once you let go of the guilt you feel about it, it will just flow to you. You block it for a reason, not because you have no time to write it, but because you are not ready yet to release it. The time will come when you are ready to face it and by the end of the year, around November time, you will have completed a huge chunk of it. In the summer months, you will be inspired to start writing again, for the sun always has this effect on you. We will be coming to you in July to encourage you to write a little and it will just go from there. For now, you must let go of any guilt you feel about not having completed it, for this just blocks the flow. Let the next few months go by without having any fears about it at all and you will notice a difference in your energy levels. When you worry about things, you get tired and this book being at the back of your mind all the time puts a huge strain on you, whether you realize it or not. Do not worry about a thing and we will complete it Mom. It will be a wonderful addition to many people's bookshelves and it will go out to the masses when the time is right. You just need to have a bit more confidence in yourself as a writer. Your writing is lovely. Perhaps you could ask one of your animal totems to come in and give you the boost and motivating energy that you need to get on with it."

"Tell Cody that I miss him and that I love him. We are still brothers in spirit and we still do many things together. I watch out for him, especially when he is out with his friends. There is a new love coming for him soon. She has blond hair and green eyes. She will be good for him and she will give him the love that he needs at this moment in time. Tell him I am with him when he is playing ball and that I could kick the ball better than him (he is laughing and he knows Cody will take this in a jokey way)." He was good at sports when he was alive, he says. I feel that he had such a competitive streak and he liked to win games, no matter what it was he was playing. I can see him give Cody a playful punch on the top of his arm and he says "dude."

I feel that Thomas is coming in now. With him, I feel a quick passing, perhaps in an automobile accident, or this is connected to him. He shows me his heart too and compression of the head. I am also getting the age of 17 connected with him. His message for you is "Hi, lovely one. You are still so beautiful, just like you were back then when we were together. You were always gorgeous and I have been told that when you were in high school, you had all the boys chasing after you all the time. You were like the nation's sweetheart – the treasure that everyone wanted. Only one lucky man got to have you and he was envied by many. You are doing so well in your spiritual life and although you say you have not really done much with it recently, you have been. You have been doing a lot of work in the spiritual realms, as you have been too busy with your earthly work to do as much as you would like in your awake state. Things will become easier for you over time and you will eventually find more time for your spirituality. You must first work on yourself, for you still have much healing to do in regard to the loss of Steven. You seem ok on the outside, but on the inside, you are still torn at the loss you feel. You know that time is a great healer, but you wonder just how much longer you can go on with this pain inside of you. Well, I can say that the pain will always be there, but you can change your mindset to deal with it more easily. The pain will lessen over time and although it has been a long time now since Steven's death, it still feels a bit raw to you. There are parts of it that have never healed within you, and now is the time to go deep down inside yourself to reach in and heal all that is still open. There are wounds that you have not been able to cover over, for the tears inside you will not allow it. You must face up to it, dear one and let the tears flow. There is much healing to be done, so let it all out and let yourself grieve. You have been trying to hold it all in and hold things together for Cody, but you must allow yourself this time to grieve too, otherwise the wounds will not heal. Just pretending that everything is ok and putting on a brave face will not heal the wounds. Yes, it can help you feel better, but to truly heal them, you must go deep inside and let yourself feel the pain, so you can release it. When I say feel the pain, I do not mean that you need to go through this pain once more. What I mean is that you need to go inside the wounds where the pain lies, and release it. It is hidden deep inside the wounds and once it has been released, the wounds can then close over and heal up. You have indeed closed and healed many wounds so far, but there are more still there. These are dotted around your heart chakra and also around your womb area, where you hold on to your connection with Steven. You controlled his birth, yet you could not control his death. He was taken from you, you feel. This is what you need to heal. It was his choice to leave the earth plane and although this is hard for you, you must accept that you could not control this, nor could you have prevented it. It was something his soul chose to go through and it was painful for him, but he got through it and he managed it so well. He done you proud, so lift your head high and know that you done your best and you done all you could to support him with his choice. You were there for him, just like you were there for him when he was born. You sent him love as he passed to spirit, just like you sent him love as he was born to earth. You done your job wonderfully, as a mother and as a friend. I am here today to help you and you can call on me anytime you wish. I may seem different to you in the way that I speak, but I am on a higher level now. I have progressed on many levels and in many ways over the years. I am at my peak and I am loving it."

In this reading I asked for a message from Steven and my friend Thomas "Tommy" that had passed away at age 18 from a motorcycle injury. He and I were really good friends since grade school. We used to walk each other home from school. On the day that I was moving to another town, he told me he wanted to ask me to go steady but he knew we could not manage it being too young to drive. I often thought of him and that sweet smile of his. It was the way he looked at me most of all that stays with me. A childhood love somehow seems more special to me than any other. It broke my heart when I learned of his accident and passing. As the family had a very private burial for him, I didn't know where he was actually buried within the huge cemetery. Shortly after, I went there and asked him to show me where he was. I heard his voice guiding me. I felt his love and the energy of him when I was at the exact spot in which he was laid to rest. I heard him say, "Stop, look to your left. But remember, I am not there, I am here, with you." Directly in front of me, to my left, was his grave marker with his name on it. They place markers like this until the head stones are complete and ready to be put in place. I know it may seem trivial to some, but for me, this was something I needed to do for myself. To bring flowers and tell him how much I had always loved him and wished him so much peace and happiness where he was. I told him how sad it made me feel that he left his life so young. At that very moment, all I felt was his warm hug. It made me smile and feel better. I kept his picture in my nightstand drawer since the day he died. I kept it there right up until I moved to California in 2013. I will never forget him.

He was someone who made an impact on my life and I am very grateful that he came through in this reading for me. It's the only time I ever asked him to connect. From time to time, I reach out myself and tell him I am thinking of him. I always send him love.

For more information about Catherine, please visit: www.angeliclight. co.uk

My sweet Thomas Stewart. He definitely stays within my heart. He was very special to me growing up. I am very thankful that he never forgot me either. I cherish his visits.

Dan Lupacchino's Story

"I first connected with Dee a few years ago, at a group meditation we both attended in Connecticut. It was pleasure getting to meet her in person as we were connected via social media for years, but never met in person. Up until that time, I really didn't know anything about her story, history or life's work. So, I was a bit surprised when she asked me to come over to her house to give her a bodywork session. I don't generally travel for my work but I felt guided to say yes.

A few days later I found myself at Dee's house where both she and her son where getting ready to transition and move to California. She showed me a around and went to what I realized was her treatment room.

I started my healing session in my normal routine and began running energy and connecting to my guides. I got about half way through her session and had to pause for moment. There standing around us, were Ascended Master Mother Mary, a team of angels and a young man all holding space for her. They looked at me with curiosity. I felt compelled to stop and mention to Dee what I was experiencing.

She smiled and laughed as she was wondering if he was going to show himself. I asked, who? A bit confused. She looked me square and the eye and asked me. "You really don't know anything about me, do you?" Truthfully, I said no. She began to tell me her story of her son Steven, and her journey into the realm of spirit.

Steven and angels stayed with us throughout the rest of the session, relaying information back and forth between Dee and myself. Its then through Steven I found out Dee was working on a book to share with the world her story of pain and triumph.

I'll never forget that day, and the presence Steven had in spirit."

For more information about Dan, visit: www.Integrativemassage works.com

Dan's favorite photo of me and Steven at Harkness.

Spirit Reading with Jennifer Shaffer

On December 30, 2015, I had a short reading with Jennifer to ask Steven for some support in writing our story. Jennifer was away on vacation at this time in Hawaii. She said she saw a beautiful rainbow before she sat down to call me. Steven immediately came through with a little girl holding a teddy bear. He said she had passed around two months prior. He went on to share that he is helping children to transition over to the other side. He said this is his purpose. He went on to talk about my book, in particular the 9th chapter. This is the last chapter of the story; it's about "The Journey Home". He said, "Thank you for chapter 9, my work in heaven (the full circle)." He went on to say that, they all have jobs up there, but he is one of the lucky ones because he gets to work with his mom. He then showed Jennifer the dream state and how we connect at that time of the day. This was profound for me because this is when I can clearly see what's coming or when Steven and I need to do more together with his guidance. Sometimes he comes just to hang out with me. I love that most of all.

Steven told Jennifer that he is very intuitive. He said he knew something a couple of days before he passed. As you know, I shared with you earlier that he had left his body a couple of days before the end came and he went home to heaven. He said, "My grandmother has this gift of intuition but she does not want to feel it. My mom has it and chooses to see and feel everything. I am so proud of my mom for that. We get to communicate because she is not afraid and she is always there. Ready to learn. Ready to listen and share her gifts."

Jennifer said, "The Rainbow is back, and is extremely vibrant. Steven throws a football into the air and a rainbow appears." She asked me to hold on for a moment so she could go outside as Steven was calling for her to do so. He then threw the football in the air and the rainbow appeared. He told her how cool it was for him to be able to do that.

Steven said, "Birds are very significant for my mom, I send them to her all the time. They talk to her. One of her nicknames is Snow White." He says with laugher in his voice.

"Please tell my mom about Chapter 2. You tell her I said, "Don't hold back on anyone's account!" Boy, did I sure know what he was referring to there. He said, "It's your story mom, it's the truth, too bad if it hurts anyone's feelings, they will get over it." Now if you knew my son, you would know what he meant by this. We do not live our lives being in the habit of saying anything to hurt another. We say it like it is with grace, dignity, and eloquence. I listened and shared the truth with love in my heart. I am sure you must have felt that in reading that chapter. At least I sure hope you did.

Steven said, "Chapter 5 is the most important chapter. The hardest and most profound. I want my mom to share her story. Tell the truth of what is was like for her when I died. I am with her when she writes this chapter. I even make sure there is tissue around for her."

Steven went on to ask me to share more information about sacred geometry and colors and energy centers and what they mean. I plan to do more of that in another book. A self-help book written with him sharing what he sees and feels in heaven that can help us here. Look for more to come on that later on.

For more information about Jennifer, please visit: www. jennifershaffer.com

Steven's Rainbow

Spirit Reading with Colby-Psychic Rebel

I met Colby a short while after I moved to California through mutual friends. We connected on Facebook but had not yet met in person. I always felt she had a beautiful energy and I looked forward to receiving my own readings with her. We met in person for the first time at her book launch party in Manhattan Beach. That same night she gave me a reading, reminding me that I needed to finish my book and to live in my light. She speaks with truth and *says it like it is* which I appreciate. I know that night was a gift and reminder to me to finish what I started and to get ready for what's to come next. She is a bright light, one that is a true channel to spirit. I asked her to connect with Steven to share his message for this book knowing he would share his love and offer yet another confirmation about our journey. I was not surprised to see what he shared with her yet it made me cry as it always does when he shines his message with so much love and light.

"Hi Denise,

So, last night Steven came to me (woke me up early) and wanted me to deliver this message to you. I hope you find it helpful."

"Dear Mom,

Mom, I know it's been a long road for you. I've watched you try and be so strong. I never meant to hurt you and I know that we are creating something so beautiful together. I am always by your side, even when you are feeling lost. When you want to give up. I am right here. Standing next to you, holding your hand and letting you know how much I love you. I see when you are having your cup of tea and just staring out the window. As if you are asking, "what more can I do"? Please know you are doing it all. You are such a hero to me and I love you so much. I love how you would look at me and wrap me in your arms. I always felt so safe in your arms.

I know you keep asking when the tears will go away, but mom, they will never cease completely because those tears are our love for one another. It's our celebration and remembrance that we shared this physical life together. I know I was stubborn, but I also love how you would call me out on my actions at times. It brings a smile to me to know that you could see everything. You always knew, we never needed words. You are still trying to find the missing pieces, but there are no missing pieces, there is just this magic that we share and I want you to know that together we are strong. Together we are learning about love in ways our souls could never have imagined. I see you in your chair, going back and forth, trying to get the words just "perfect". They are perfect. This is our story, your story and together we write this story to share. I am giving you a rose. Today is a rose for you. I want you to hold this rose close to your heart and know that I love you with everything that I am and please keep talking to me. I can hear you. I will always be with you mom. Always."

Love,
Steven

For more information about Colby, please visit: www.psychicrebel.com

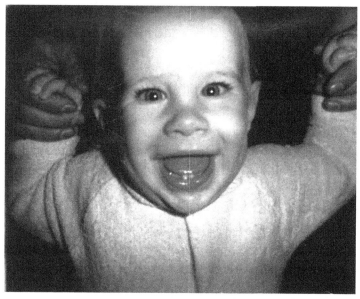

Steven's favorite photo of himself. It was his first day learning to walk. He told Colby that he wanted this one to be shared with her reading. He described it in full detail.

Spirit Reading with Margo Mateas

"I just love being with Steven because he is ALWAYS so joyful. He is always in a great mood: playful and wise, keyed into greater mysteries, but never taking anything, {including death} too seriously. He always refers to me as "buddy," and I know that we have had lifetimes together.

The day after Denise invited me to be part of this book, Steven showed me a favorite scene from his childhood: ice-skating in a winter wonderland. As it was late December, it made sense that he would choose a memory from this time of year. The setting was truly magical: holiday lights, carolers, snow, all capped off by an enormous Christmas tree decked out in full holiday splendor. I could feel his joy as he made circle after circle around the rink, his legs pumping faster and faster, throwing his head back so that all he could see were the bright lights of the Christmas tree above him in the night sky. He really felt like he was flying, soaring above the clouds, his senses immersed in twinkling stars as his heart and soul filled with absolute joy.

I texted Denise and asked if Steven ever went ice-skating in a place like this. She confirmed that she knew exactly the place he had shown me. She said it was his favorite place to go in Connecticut at Christmastime, and that he absolutely loved to go there, and would skate for hours on end.

I asked Steven what he wanted me to tell people about what he is doing now, and he says that he is working with other children stricken with leukemia. He shows himself coming into the hospital rooms to be with the children who are undergoing treatment, and also helping to shepherd them once they cross over. I can see him helping them to understand what has happened to them, where they are now, and what they will be doing next. He told me that he is mostly concerned for the parents as they try and recover the broken pieces of their hearts and go on. "I really feel badly for them. Their pain is so enormous -- like my Mom's pain," he said. "That was intense. Really intense." He goes quiet for a moment, remembering how overwhelming it was for her, how his death left her in pieces, and how the pieces are just starting to mend together now, all these years later."

Steven's Message To Parents

"Bouncing back to his ebullient self, he says, "I REALLY want the parents to know that they are never, ever alone through any of this. The minute you step through that hospital door, or even when you first get the diagnosis, angels like me are there with you. There are bigger angels, too, healing angels and angels like that, but there are lots of angels like me around, too. We send light and healing to the kids, but we also send healing to the hearts of the loved ones. Their grief is so enormous that we actually take shifts sending them light and healing, because they need so much healing for such a long time. But its okay, because we never want to leave even <u>one</u> family member feeling as if they are not loved too – because they are. As I watch a child prepare to leave his family, I KNOW that he is soon going to be fine – whole, happy and free again, with no pain of any kind. It's the ones left behind who need the most help." His heart swells with compassion, and I can feel how deeply committed he is to alleviating the emotional suffering of those affected by this disease.""

"The biggest thing for parents to remember, Steven says, is NOT TO BLAME YOURSELVES. "You didn't give your child cancer. It's not your fault. You didn't fail. You couldn't have stopped it, and you couldn't stop Death from coming. The children who die from this disease are supposed to die from it. That doesn't mean that you can't or shouldn't do everything you can to fight it – because some ARE meant to live and learn from the experience, and others are meant to come Home so they can offer the kind of angelic love and support I'm talking about – but it's not your decision. I know it's hard, but you have to forgive yourselves. As much as you love your child, it's not up to you. Give yourselves a break. You're not God. If you were, your child wouldn't be dying, right? The best you can do is to be there for all of it and realize that you are not in charge. There is a bigger Plan at work. I'm part of it, and you are part of it and your child is part of it, too. But please, don't blame yourselves. It makes it so much harder."

Steven's Message to Siblings of Children with Cancer

"At this point, Steven wants to talk about the siblings as the entire family's attention, love and resources are shifted onto the sick child. "It's really sad how the brothers and sisters of really sick kids get left out. It's like they don't exist anymore. They feel sad and scared that they're going to lose a brother or sister; they don't know what to do about their feelings; they feel terrified to say anything and never know what to say, so they don't say anything at all, and basically, they just try to make themselves go away so they don't cause any trouble and the family can keep focusing on the child who is sick."

"But dudes!" he exclaims in the California surfer lingo I find so endearing, "be there for yourselves! You matter too! You can't stop living because someone else is dying. You have to live the life you are given, and don't feel bad about it. Don't feel guilty. Life chose YOU to keep on going, to have a life on Earth and to blossom and be what you are supposed to be. So please – don't stop living while a loved one is dying. Don't live like you're holding your breath all the time, because that is like dying, too. You're only allowing yourself enough air to just stay alive, like you don't feel worthy to take a big gulp of the stuff and really live. It's okay to live. Really, it's okay to live. We <u>all</u> want <u>you</u> to live."

Steven's Message to Parents About How to Help Siblings Cope

"The hardest thing a parent will ever do is bury a child. That's just a fact. There's no getting around it. It's the most horrible thing that could ever happen. How can you continue to love and keep life going on as normal, when all of this is going on? Obviously, you can't. But this is what Steven wants you to do for the children who are still with you:"

1) "You gotta spend time ALONE with your living kids and give them lots of eye contact and snuggles (even if they're teens). They need your love now more than ever, because they just found out that you can be young and still die, and that is really scary. They also need to know that they still matter to you. And they should, because the ones you get to keep are just as important as the ones you lose. Tell them you love them and you're so glad you're all going through this together."

2) "You gotta give them permission to live, even though someone else is dying. Keep their life going as much as you can (I know that's almost impossible, but do the best you can) with everyday activities and friends and stuff like that. Let them have days off where they can just be normal for a little while and forget about everything. And don't resent them for being able to forget for a little while, even though you can't. They're kids. That's what they have to do."

3) "You gotta acknowledge that this sucks, and that you are sorry that you can't be in their lives right now like you

were before, but that you <u>WILL BE AGAIN</u> once this is over. At some point, it will be "over" and life will go on. But you have to tell your healthy kids that you know you're not there for them as much as you want to be, but that THEY still matter while this is going on, and that you will be there for them later. Of course, nothing is ever going to go back to the way it was, but at least staying connected to your other kids will create a bond between you that will be stronger than it was before, because you have gone through all this together and didn't break apart. You clung together instead of shutting down and isolating yourself and making everyone try to find a way of coping on their own."

Steven's Message About Keeping the Family Together During Times of Stress

"Come together. Be together. Open up your love and wrap it all the way around everyone in the family. All of you. All in, together. That's the way to get through this. If you don't, it will kill you. It will kill your souls, and then you will all be just as dead as the child you lost. Don't die. Don't let your family die. I know you can't control how everyone will react, but they all will look to you for how to handle it: what to say, how much they can express, what's allowed and what's not. Open it all up. Open it up to everything. Make that expression circle as big as the Universe. Let everything in, and let everything out. Make everything okay. Give everyone tons of space, but squeeze tight to bring everyone back together, too. That way no one has to feel shut out or left behind or like they are not important any more."

"This is very key, because stress and death break families apart. And we are all one big Universal family. So, it's very important that you do this as best you can. It should make you feel better and lighter, because you won't have to police everyone and try and guard what they say or how they feel. Just let go of all that -- and let everyone be who they are and keeping loving them anyway, even though it's scary because you think you might lose them, too. Keep loving. Keep love in the family. Keep love in all your relationships, as much as possible. Some people will go away because they can't handle it, but that's okay. Keep loving anyway."

"We are ALL one in this Universal Family, and everyone is loved equally. That's the biggest difference between here and there… here; everything is Love, all the time. You are never without it. It's always here, just like breathing is where you are. It's all around us, and we can never, ever feel separate or unwhole or anything like that. It feels really, really good. And that's why we all feel so badly for the families. So, families, you need to band together. You need to go to support groups. You need to hold onto each other. Keep your heart open to all the love you can find – and open up to me and the angels who are around you all the time. We are there for the whole family, not just the one who is dying."

Steven's Message about Angels and the Circle of Life

"It's a big, beautiful circle of Life. The ones who pass over come and check on the ones who are heading out, and then they come back and become Watchers over the next set. It's a big, continuous circle of love and healing that never, ever stops. So, when you are on the brink of despair, look up and around in that hospital room, or wherever you are, and know that we are there. If you can see clairvoyantly, look for us – because we are always there."

"I'm not an archangel, so I can't be everyone at once like they can. I have certain cases that are assigned to me (Heaven is more businesslike than you think), and sometimes we don't know who is going to be crossing over, until the beginning of the end. That's why it's important to have hope as long as you can, because Hope protects your heart. It's like having a superhero shield over you. Hope can lift you up, keep you strong and keep you from breaking apart – so hold onto it as long as you can."

"Don't be afraid to talk about death, either. Let your loved ones know that a beautiful LIFE awaits them on the Other Side."

"Steven could go on talking like this for hours. His spirit is an effervescent fountain of optimism and light. When I ask him how he wants to leave this chapter, he smiles and says with a happy, contented sigh:"

"It's all good. It really is."

For more information about Margo, please visit: www.margomateas.com

Steven at Hubbard Park. His favorite place to feed the
ducks, ice skate, and tour the holiday lights at Christmas
time. He chose this photo to go along with Margo's reading.
He told her all about his ice skating days there.

Dragana's Story

"The moment I met Denise, I felt a sense of recognition. I
was drawn to her light, strength of presence and sparkle in
her eyes. We met at a Reiki Sound event I was facilitating.
It was during the session when I came beside her to give
Reiki that I felt a sense of reverence. I knew I was in the
presence of a deep profound spiritual teacher surrounded
in Angelic love. Intuitively, I knew she had been through
so much, I sensed that she had experienced deep pain
that was birthing a profound message that needed to be
shared with the world. I connected deeply on a soul level
with Denise and share a love for the Angelic realm that
surrounds her."

For more information about Dragana Gobic, please email her at: draganagobic@msn.com

Kendra's Story

"I had the pleasure of meeting Denise many years ago on the east coast and we immediately became friends. Our paths crossed when she took a job at a place I had been working at for a few years. We immediately connected and I noticed instantly how warm and loving she is. I also noticed that there was something very special about her, but wasn't quite sure what it was at the time. She exuded peacefulness; light and love that really made me feel very safe when I spoke with her.

Fast forward a few years later, I relocated back to the west coast and Denise's healing practice was growing incredibly fast. I had recently been through some major life changes and was in need of some healing and to get back in balance. It was a time in my life where I was doing a lot of growing spiritually and it was a challenge to stay in balance. At the time, I was still fighting adrenal fatigue and feeling the effects that come with it, exhaustion, foggy mind, feelings of being ungrounded and persistent dizziness.

When I arrived that afternoon, Denise intuitively knew which healing would benefit me and my situation. She suggested "Stevens's Gift". I was excited as I knew this was a very special healing.

When I arrived at her office location, I immediately felt peaceful. It was as if the stresses I was dealing with had already begun to fade away. She spent some time before the session speaking with me about what was going on in my life and how I was currently feeling. It was often before the words tumbled out that she already knew how I felt.

Once in the healing room, I noticed soft and beautiful music playing. Once on the table it was slightly warm and incredibly comfortable. As Denise organized the oils, all of which she custom makes and charges with healing energy, we spoke a little. The day before as I was developing some of my own custom oil blends, I came up with one of the names as gilded. As we spoke and she began the healing she said to imagine that the angels were all waiting at the gilded gate. Then she said gilded again. I said why did you say gilded? I had told no one that that word was in my head for the past few days. She said that Steven told her to say it and she said, "Okay". Steven giggled as he knew that that word was important to me. As soon as Denise said that the angels were present at the gilded gate, I felt enveloped in love and protection. As soon as Denise began to spray the oils, I was taken aback by how absolutely beautiful, and heavenly they were. My immediate observation was that that these oils were very sacred, special and of a very high vibration. As the healing began to progress along with the healing massage, my mind was quiet and I had an out of body experience but yet at the same time I felt grounded in my experience and was very much present. Denise used a few different oils on my feet to ground me and that was apparent during the healing in the way that I felt. The healing was like nothing I have ever experienced. At the end of the healing I felt rebalanced, healed and incredibly peaceful, but also filled with love. Renewed and balanced I headed out to enjoy the day. At the beginning of the healing Denise explained that at the end of her healing sessions she likes for her clients to be in their light and go on their way after so that is exactly what I did and it was magical. I feel blessed and grateful to have been fortunate enough that Denise shared her gifts with me. It was an incredibly divine and sacred experience."

For more information about Kendra Amos, please visit: www. beloveflow.com

Chapter 9

The Journey Home

I am so very excited to write this last chapter. To me, it's not the end, but more so, the beginning of everything new that has become part of my new existence. My new life. Onwards and upwards onto my new path fully living my true life's purpose. This is exactly where I belong.

Today is May 10, 2017. It's taken me a very long time to get to this chapter. I often wondered when, if at all, this book might actually come to fruition. Each time I was guided to write, it seemed that only certain aspects were coming through and I was reminded that my journey was still unfolding. I had no idea how long it was going to take for me to make peace with the loss of my son. In all that I have learned about myself and about my connection to him and heaven, I still questioned how long my heart would ache with missing his physical presence. Honestly, it's been almost 14 years now and I still miss him the same as I did from the moment he left his body. One thing is for certain, I have made peace with this and I no longer have the pain in my heart that I felt back then. I wish I could say that time does heal all wounds, but in the loss of a child, time does not fully heal this heartbreaking loss. What time actually does is help us to grow and to move forward so that we can live our lives. I do a lot in honor of Steven and I also do a lot for me. Steven reminds me every day that he wants me to be happy. He wants me to live my very best life. I used to rely on that support to help me get through the tough days. I've learned how to survive and take care of myself without feeling like I need a crutch to lean on. This took quite some time. But I did it. I live it every day. It sounds simplistic to say, *live your dreams* but to me, this is the motto that helped me push through the darkness and come back to the light. If I can do this, so can you. Everyone can. You just have to have faith in yourself. Believe in yourself. Love yourself. Nurture yourself. Just be the love that you are. That's it. It's that simple.

In the summer of 2011 I just had my beautiful in ground pool opened. All of my perennial gardens were in full bloom and the house and the yard looked gorgeous. So many years of planting things and watching them multiply seemed to have finally paid off. Only inside, I felt like something was still missing in my life. Cody was going to be graduating in 2013 so I knew it was time to make some changes in my life. I just didn't know what that was going to be just quite yet. We planned a trip to San Diego to visit our cousins. I had not been there since I was in my 20's. Something told me that Cody might really love it as much as I did. After all, it was a place that was perfectly aligned to him and his love of the outdoors. I knew he would fit right in with everyone. We had an amazing time exploring places and just laughing and enjoying ourselves. He repeatedly mentioned how much he loved it there. Once our trip was over and our flight landed back home in Connecticut, both he and my niece were miserable. I smiled to myself as I know quite well the effect California has on one's soul. The next few words out of his mouth were, "This sucks Mom… Welcome back to suck town." I laughed and said, "See? I told you it's amazing out there, nothing like the life we live here. Maybe we should just sell the house and move there." This made him perk his head up with a look of shock on his face. He responded, "Let's do it." I said, "Okay. We'll make another trip next year to look at colleges and get things in motion. There is no turning back now. You said it and now we are doing it." And that's exactly what we did. I had thought about my connection to California and wondered if that was really where I was meant to be. I had felt that I had lived there in another time and I questioned if I was just trying to possibly live out what I had started during that lifetime. Whenever I thought about it, I felt excited at the thought of planning a future there. That made me want to believe that it was about the future and not a past journey. And so, we set our plans in motion.

In 2012, we went back to California and checked out colleges and spent a lot of time sight-seeing. It was one of my most favorite trips. It felt so good knowing that we were on our way to making this huge life change. For both of us. On the last day of our trip, we were in Hollywood. We seemed to gravitate to the Hollywood hills since we had first arrived. We kept going back there instead of venturing to other places. As we were making a mad dash to get to the car and head to the airport, I had this feeling in my chest, an overwhelming sense of anxiety, only not in a bad way. I've never felt this way before. I felt like there something I was supposed to pay attention to but didn't know what it might be. Then I heard Steven say, "Look up Mom. Look behind you." I noticed a white building; I could see part of it at the top of the hill. I asked my friend Amy what she thought it might be. I told her that I needed to go there right now. She reminded me that we had to be on the road to the airport or we would miss our flight. Now the panic was sinking in. I had to go there. *What is that place, why is it calling me like a beacon in the night?* I heard Steven say, "Mom, you know what it is, it's the observatory. Don't worry, you will be back soon. You can see it then." I tried to let it go, to just focus on getting home and making my plans for my next trip. It stayed with me. I had dreams about it. I felt like it was a place I had been to before. When I got home I immediately went on the computer to research it. Then I remembered where I knew it from. Since I was a kid, I had a love for James Dean and his movies. Especially *Rebel Without A Cause*. As I was researching this, I heard a bang on the window screen. It was around 10pm so it startled me a bit. I looked to my right and saw a large red cardinal hanging onto the screen with its claws. It was the biggest cardinal I had ever seen. Its yellow eyes were focused right on mine. We just stared at each other for what seemed like an eternity. I could not help but say, "Well? What are you trying to tell me? Is that all you've got?" It flew away, and to this day, I am not sure what that was all about. I just knew it had a meaning and I took that as a sign that there was much more to come.

In April of 2013 I noticed that my beloved dog Kelsey was looking a little tired. She always perked herself up when Cody and I were home and still ran to greet us at the door. At this time, she was no longer doing that and I knew it might be time for her to go home to heaven. I didn't want her to, I loved her so much and I just could not imagine our life in California without her. Cody told me that he thought that she needed to stay here, at her home and was getting too old to make such a big move. He reassured me that Steven would be with her to take care of her. I begged him not to say those words, to not even put the thought out there. But deep down I knew he was right. I had an event at my house one night and she kept coming over to me barking as if she was trying to tell me something. I knew she felt a lot of spirits around as I was giving healings and angel card readings for a group of people that had loved ones on the other side. She normally would just lie by my feet or under my healing table but on this night, she kept barking at me trying to get me to pay attention to her. I had a feeling it was her way of telling me that Steven was here with her and that she wanted to go with him but my fear of losing her would not allow me to listen to her. I held her and tried to push the thought away.

The next morning when I woke up, she was asleep by my side. I cuddled her and kissed her head to wake her so she could have some time outside before I left for the office. When she came back in from outside I had this overwhelming feeling that I should stay home with her. I felt fear clutch my heart and then I heard Steven say, "It's okay Mom, I've got her, just go to work. They need you today." It happened to be a day in which I had to handle the support center calls as the others were on vacation. I picked her up to hold her close and told her how much we loved her and thanked her for being such a wonderful care giver to all of us. I thanked her for loving us so much and for taking extra special care of Steven when he was sick. I told her it was okay if she wanted to go home and be with her Steven. I then told her that when she was ready to go, to please make it an easy transition for Cody and me as we did not want to see her become ill or in pain in any way, shape or form. I kissed her sweet face and put her down and watched her as she walked into my spa room to lie down. This was my sign that she was going to the room of love, light and healing. I prayed for peace for all of us. It was spring break so Cody was asleep in his room when I left. I got to the office and tried to focus and not worry. I could not stop the feelings from coming. Cody called me to say something was wrong with Kelsey. He said she went to the bathroom in the house and seemed out of it. He was scared. I told him to pick her up and to hold her and take her to bed with him while he played his video games so she would not be alone. He wrapped her in his favorite blanked and said she went to sleep. About an hour later he called me freaking out and said,

"Mom, Kelsey just died! Mom please come home now I can't handle this." My heart burst into a billion tiny pieces. I could not control the tears that came and my friends that I worked with were so wonderful, they didn't want me to drive but I assured them I would be okay once I got to my Jeep. I told our boss I had to leave and she said it was okay and that they would all pitch in and handle the support calls. I prayed it would be a light day as I did not want to burden anyone with my responsibility. I ran outside and called my friend Cliff. He and I were supposed to have lunch together that day. I was crying so hard that I could not talk, I could only say that I needed him and to please meet me at my house. He responded, "On my way honey." I called my mom and my best friend while driving home. I needed them as I had not expected the devastation to hit me that hard. It was so similar to how I felt when my Steven died. All I felt was an intense, very painful, deep pain in my heart.

As soon as I arrived home, Cody was in the kitchen waiting for me, he was afraid to go back to his room. I felt so bad that he was there alone when this happened. I thanked him for taking care of her and I ran down the stairs to his room to be with her. As soon as I saw her lifeless body, I screamed out in pain. Cody came running down the stairs trying so hard to fight back his tears and he just hugged me as I sobbed. It was awful. I never wanted my children to see me in pain let alone cry like this. I am the strong one, the "go-to" person, not the one who needs the help. The doorbell rang and I knew it would be Cliff. I told Cody to go upstairs and get shovels ready as we were going to bury her in her favorite garden. I ran up the stairs to hug Cliff and to thank him for coming. At this point he still had no idea what was wrong but he had a feeling. He said, "Did Kelsey die?" I cried and nodded yes. It broke my heart to put all of this emotion on those I loved and cared so much for. But I knew that my friends and family loved me and were happy to be with me, to do whatever I needed just as I had always done for them. It meant the world to me. I asked him to dig a very deep hole so we could bury her and not have to worry about any animals digging her up. She was only 14 pounds but I still felt better in knowing that she had a proper burial deep within the earth. I ran back downstairs to get her and held her in my arms. I could not stop the crying. I just loved her so much.

I thanked Steven for coming to be with her and take her home. I prayed for the strength to be able to make it back up the stairs as I felt my legs giving out. I sat down holding her and rocking her on the patio watching Cliff and Cody digging the hole. When they were done, I asked Cody to go inside and get Steven's favorite sweatshirt, the one she used to pull down from where I kept it hanging on my bedroom closet door handle. She always made it into a little bed for herself. It seemed like the best way for me to honor her and Steven in this way. My mom and my friend Karen had just arrived, running to hug me while I clutched onto my sweet girl. I knew they felt my pain as it equally showed upon their faces. A mirror image of what I was feeling inside. My mom touched Kelsey's head and said, "Dee Dee, she is so warm, are you sure she is gone?" I said, "Yes Mom, she's gone, you are feeling my energy surrounding her with love and light. It's okay, don't be alarmed by it." It took all my strength to physically stand up. I was still crying and had a hard time in keeping my body from crumbling into a heap on the ground. The hole was too deep for me to reach into so I handed our girl over to Cody to have him and Cliff place her in the ground. I knew this was hard for him but it had to be done this way. My tears were blurring my eyes but it was hard to not see the colors all around her. Pink, white, and soft purple all blended together and covered her in a blanket of light. I knew the angels were with her and I knew that she was being surrounded in their blanket of abundant love. I lit a candle and placed it upon her grave and I said a prayer before we all went inside the house. It was beautiful and yet completely heart breaking. It gave me peace in knowing that she was in her favorite garden.

We drank champagne to celebrate and honor her life. We watched movies that brought us joy and comfort. My niece came over and we took Cody shopping and then he went to hang out with his friends. Once everyone went home, my mom and I made tea and watched a movie together before going to bed. I was exhausted. I was devastated and still the tears kept coming. Later that night I felt someone at the foot of my bed. I knew it was my son. He said, "I brought you a special surprise mom." I felt him standing there holding Kelsey in his arms and then he put her on my bed. She ran over to where I was laying, I started to cry harder as she was running all around me just like she did when she was alive. I felt her nose sniffing my ear and when I didn't turn towards her, she ran around my body to kiss my face. This only made me cry harder. Steven said, "Its okay Mom, she is with me now." I then felt him scoop her up and they laid next to me on the bed. The two of them stayed with me till I fell asleep. When the morning sun came to wake me, I felt peaceful. I felt incredibly blessed to have such a connection with my son and I was so thankful that he did this for me. I prayed the peace would stay with me to take away the sadness I felt.

A couple days later, I found another shirt I liked to put on when I hung out at home. I needed a replacement to Steven's sweatshirt and didn't want to go through his clothes to find another. I wore this shirt all day as I went out shopping with Cody to find an angel for Kelsey's grave. We bought flowers and planted them in her garden. It looked gorgeous. The butterflies and the birds seemed to notice as they all came by to visit that day. This made my heart happy. As I was getting ready for bed, I hung the shirt on the bedroom closet door handle and lit a candle asking the angels to help me sleep peacefully. I fell fast asleep and woke up to the sun the following morning. As it was the weekend, I wanted to get up early and run some errands. When I came home, that white shirt was on the floor, in a circle shape, the very same shape that Kelsey used to do with Steven's sweatshirt. As my house was always super tidy with everything in its place, this was the only thing on the floor and no one was home that day except for me, so I knew it was her. She was here, hanging out in her room. I felt bad as I needed to take all of her things out of the house the night of her passing as I could not bear to see them. I wondered if she was upset that her things were gone when she came to visit. I quickly let those feelings go when I looked down at the shirt again. She reminded me that she always preferred to sleep on our clothes anyway. I left that shirt there for a couple days. If there was ever any doubt I had in questioning that our pets actually do visit us after they are gone was certainly vanished from my mind after that day. I questioned this no longer.

In June of 2013, Cody was finally getting ready to graduate high school. I thought the day would never come! I began connecting to recruiters in California and applied to all the positions I knew would be a great match for me. I had an amazing connection to a man named Sean. He and I talked on the phone for a long time and I just knew he and I were connected by the angels. He called me a couple days later with great news. I had been presented to a company that he was working with and they were looking forward to meeting me in person. Once they learned I lived in Connecticut, they informed Sean that they wanted someone local, even after he told them I was not expecting their help in making the move out to California if I had been given the position. They chose a local candidate anyway. I did not let this defeat me and told him that we should not put my address on my resume any longer and just put my email address on it. So that's what we did. Summer was coming to an end and one day when I was lounging on a raft in my pool, all by myself, I thought, *this just has to be my last summer here, I need to get back home. I need to start my next chapter of my life. I cannot ever have that here. This past life is over. Please help me make this happen.*

Fall came and things were moving slowly. I put off closing the pool for as long as I could. The first week of October, the pool guy came over shaking his head. He said, "Denise... you are ALWAYS the last one on the list to close the dang pool, what's the deal, even with the heater it's still too cold out here to use it anyway, what gives?" I laughed and said, "Vin, I LIVE for summer, the flowers, the birds, the bees, the butterflies, being outside all the time is what makes me feel alive and happy. Once you guys arrive and close up the pretty blue and sparkly water, I know it's going to be a long 8 to 9 months of cold, crappy days and I hate looking out the window and seeing that pool cover for so damn long. It makes me unhappy. Summer is just too short. So, I keep it open to keep my spirit alive." He just shook his head as he walked away to get the process started and then he stopped and turned to look my way and said, "You are living in the wrong state lady. This is Connecticut you know. Summers are hot and short lived." He then smiled and went back to work. Under my breath I responded, "No shit summers are short, story of my life... soon to be a thing of the past. Peace OUT Connecticut... See ya later alligator!" And then I went into the house to search for more jobs. This process continued every night all throughout the weekends. I had to stop myself as it was becoming too much. I knew I needed to have faith and that it would happen when the timing was exactly right. I prayed it would be before the snow started to fall. I basically begged the angels for their help. Cody asked at least once a week, "Mom, when are we moving? It's almost winter. I thought you said we would be out of here by fall." I responded, "We will be. Keep praying and picturing yourself there. Don't give up on it. I am working with recruiters and I know it's almost time. Soon. You'll see."

On the night of Thursday, September 26th, my recruiter friend Sean called with great news. There was so much happiness in his voice when he said he found the perfect job for me to start with in California. After he told me all about it, I told him that it sounded perfect for me and to go ahead and submit me. He said, "I knew you would say that so I already did. I expect to hear from the hiring manager in the morning." And that he did. He called me the next day to tell me they loved my resume and my background and were excited to have me in for an interview. I was at the top of their list. This was to be an eighteenth month contract which paid decent so I could manage my new life out there and get things moving in the right direction. I told him to set it up ASAP and to be sure that they had no idea I was living in Connecticut. We were not going to risk losing another job to that little oversight. About 5 minutes after I hung up with him, another recruiter in his office called me for another position at the same company. So, they presented me for both. I was to interview on the following Monday for both positions. One at 9am and the other in the afternoon at 1pm. I called my travel agent and booked a flight out for two days. I had plenty of time to get myself ready and be there refreshed and ready to go. The interview was great. The campus the company was on was incredibly beautiful so I knew this was going to work out for me. As soon as I finished and got in the car to head out and sight see, Sean called and said I had the job and they wanted me to start in two weeks! What??? I was able to push for 3 weeks which meant I needed to really work hard to get my house of fourteen+ years in order to be staged and sold and also to pack up for our new life in California.

What a whirlwind this would be. I didn't even go for the other interview as both Sean and I didn't want to miss any offers on the table by taking any chances. I was so excited. I immediately went to Starbucks, ordered a latte and changed my clothes in the bathroom. Since it was only 10:30am, I still had the whole day and night to sight see and enjoy myself in this place that called to my heart so deeply. I drove everywhere, walked along the beach in Malibu, toured the canyon, shopped in Westlake Village and made my way to the Hollywood hills. I wanted to spend the night watching the sun set in those hills and the first stop on my list was the Griffith Observatory. I knew it was closed as it was a Monday. But I didn't care. I could barely breathe while driving ever so slowly up that windy hill to get there. It was incredible. It took all I had in me to keep myself grounded as I felt like I was floating; the energy around me and within me just seemed to buzz. I never felt this way before. It was like stepping into the land of euphoria. I was beyond elated to be there. There was no one there which seemed odd to me, but I took that as a sign that I was meant to be there taking it all in on my own. A gift, if you will, just for me. I took in a deep breath before heading over to the stairs that led to the front door of this magical place. I put my hands on them and closed my eyes. I could feel so much energy from all those that had entered through the front doors over the many years since the place was built. I felt like I was in heaven.

I walked all around the place and made my way to the back driveway, the place where James Dean once stood while filming *Rebel Without A Cause*. It made me catch my breath as I stood where he stood near the wall that overlooks Los Angeles. I closed my eyes so I could take it all in. Every ounce of me was flying high to the sky... the air up there feels magical, so full of hopes and dreams. *The City of Angels*. This is how I feel about this place. I could not stop smiling from the inside out. I took pictures of everything to commemorate this trip, to capture the beginning of my new life on film as to never forget a single moment. I walked back to the front of the building and was drawn to the statue there. Then I remembered that I read something many years ago that there was a memorial statue there in honor of James Dean. A beautiful statue of just his head capturing that smile of his. I walked over to it and took a photo before touching his face softly. I heard Steven say, "Look at the time." It was 5:45pm. I felt an instant whoosh type of feeling come over me, as if I was taken back in time for a brief moment. It was intense. And then it came back to me. "Oh, My God", I said aloud, "Today is September 30th. James Dean was killed in a car accident on this day at 5:45pm. What the hell? What does this even mean? Why am I here right now? At this exact time?" It was an intense sensation that ran through me. I had to sit down and just breathe. I stayed there, in that spot till the sky started to turn pink. I knew the sun would be setting soon so I reluctantly made my way back to the car and slowly made my way back to Hollywood. I took a drive and found a place that had amazing tacos and hung out till it was time to head to LAX and take a red eye flight back to Connecticut.

My beloved Griffith Observatory. I took this on September 30th, 2013. It was my very first visit there. My first of many!

I was so excited on the flight home, going through all the things that I needed to do in order to prepare my house for sale and to clean out the home I had lived in with my family for so long. I had amazing friends and family helping me through this process. Two very special friends came to help me go through all of Steven's things. I knew he was there too as it was not hard nor was it sad for me at all. I put some things of Steven's aside that I wanted to keep and when Cody came home, he selected some things to keep for himself as well. This made me happy. It was a lot of work but it was so easy to release the house as we were so ready to make a new life for ourselves. We had a big party to say good bye to everyone.

We were so excited and I know that most were happy and equally as excited for us. The others were sad but I knew this was how it would be. Not everyone could understand why we needed to do this. Then the final day came and while I was packing, I was on the phone making all the arrangements for our new place to live. It's a good thing I am great at multitasking. I was even seeing clients at night and on the weekends and working full time right up until the day before we left! But we did it. We packed everything up, put it all at a friend's house and when the car carrier company arrived, they allowed my friends to put all the boxes in the Jeep too. Cody and I left with two suitcases full each and two jam packed carry-on bags and we boarded our one-way flight to LAX. We were so excited as the plane was descending into LAX. And then it wasn't. Wait, what? There was a shooting at the airport that day; an employee who lost his edge literally had the entire airport shut down. Our flight was rerouted to Vegas. No problem. Who's tired? Not us, we've got this. We waited for hours to see when flights would be going back to LAX. They finally released all the luggage so we grabbed two carts and our bags and ran as fast as we could to the car rental place. Since I already had a car rented for the week ready and waiting for me at LAX, it took a while to redo the paperwork so I could take a car from Vegas instead. The line was beyond long but we did it. We got in the car, made the five-hour drive, checked into a hotel and moved into our place in the morning. Were we tired? You cannot even begin to imagine how tired we were having not really slept in weeks. My cousins came up to stay overnight with us to welcome us home. We had a good time and they helped us set up our new place. I guess I should have listened to my inner voice when I was that tired to take a break and rest. But no... I just had to have things organized for us so it would be cozy for Cody. I cut my hand pretty bad. Bad enough that I needed to have a lot of stitches from the inside out. Not an easy feat to find a hospital at 1am. But we did. Another challenge checked off the list. We were on our way and we were ready to embrace whatever was to come next.

We literally arrived in California with just a few days to settle in before I started my new job. It was so exciting. We quickly shopped and bought things to make our place homey. I knew the transition would be tough for us but we were ready. It also brought Cody and me together in a way that we had not shared before. He made friends and had fun at the skate park which was down the street from our place. It took some time but he eventually started to feel more at home. I can't say we were truly homesick although we did miss our friends. Inside, I knew that the new friends that we had yet to meet were going to become the best friends of our lives, the ones that we would share life together with until we went home to heaven. I felt this deeply within my heart and soul.

We were only in California a couple months when Cody asked to go to CT for his Christmas gift so he could see his friends and cousins. I didn't mind at all so he went there in January so we could spend our first Christmas in our new home. We kept it light that year as I knew he was having a tough time getting himself settled. Soon after the New Year he made friends and got a job so life was progressing onward. One day he asked if we could get a puppy. I didn't want to have any more pets as this move was meant to make both of our lives more carefree and easier without adding in any more responsibilities. He kept at it though, and he constantly reminded me of how much he hated a home without a dog. I understood that quite well. He had just turned 18 the summer before we moved so I thought it was a good idea for him to have a companion. After all, dogs are the best at giving unconditional love. And we both sure do love dogs. We agreed to come up with a happy medium. I wanted a Jack Russell Terrier and he wanted a Mini Pincher. So, I reached out to all the shelters and we put our name on the list for the right dog for us. On February 8th, I received a call from a woman who had just received a mom and her three pups. She described them to me over the phone. In my heart, I knew that one of the little girls was for us. Without even seeing a picture yet, I just felt it. Once the picture was emailed to me, it was confirmed for me. I called the woman right away and told her to please hold the puppy that she referred to as "Lovey". Since Cody was sleeping over his friend Josh's house, I had to do this on my own. I knew he would not mind as I knew what he wanted.

In the morning, the woman's husband and daughter came over with a truck carrying with them a few different sets of puppies in carriers. They were out making their rounds to show off the pups to all the people that were waiting to see them all. They placed a pen on the ground and took the first two of Lovey's siblings out and placed them in the pen so I could see them all before making my selection. I was standing near the truck watching them when the man reached into the little carrier and pulled out Lovey. As soon as he had her in his arms, she saw me and started crying and wagging her tail and trying to get away from him to get to me. He said, "Oh my God, I've never seen a puppy do this before. It's like she already knows you." As soon as he said those words she jumped from his arms into mine, all the while kissing my neck, my face, my arms, and my chest still yelping and crying out with excitement. It nearly brought me to my knees. This tiny, less than 3 pounds, little puppy that I had never seen before had captured my heart and I knew she was my Kelsey. I cried out and she cried out so the man and his daughter started crying and he then said, *"I think this one is for you."* I could only nod my head yes. I could not put her down for even a second. They gave me her food, bowls, paperwork, etc. and I paid them and took her into the house to grab a towel so I could take her to the store to get a crate, a bed, treats and toys. I even bought her a name tag with my cell number on it. I was elated. As was Cody when he first saw her. I picked him up and as soon as I handed her to him he cried and said, *"Mom, I love her."* And that was that. Our little girl made her way back to us. We were so happy. Our girl did come home to California with us after all. We named her Lucy Lu. Our sweet little Jack Russell Terrier Mix. She is black and white, the perfect mix for what we both had wished for.

Lucy Lu and Cody

The following month, in March, Cody's girlfriend came out to surprise him. They had started dating towards the end of their senior year. It was so great to see his face light up when she walked into the room without him knowing anything of her trip. I picked her up at the airport and she immediately fell in love with California just as I knew she would. To see his face when she walked in the room was priceless. They had a great time and they made plans for her to come out and visit when she was on summer break from school. I knew it was hard for them to be apart but I had not expected that Cody would want to go back to Connecticut with her in the fall after she went home. She was not even gone two weeks and he was miserable so I told him he should do what he felt was right for him. He took a one-way flight back to Connecticut and they tried to make things work. She was living at home with her parents and he was staying with friends. I knew he was miserable and wanted to come home to California. I did my best to just send love and light every day and to be there for him when he needed to talk. She was working and going to school and he was just hanging out. I prayed things would evolve in some way so that he would be happy.

This time was very hard for me as I was completely alone for the first time in my life. I felt like I was grieving again and some of those old painful feelings erupted and almost crushed me to my core. I had to work hard to connect within and heal myself. I had to go deep to remind myself that I was on my own journey too and it was important that I stay on track not only for me, but for Cody and all those I was yet to meet and have the gift of working with. I just felt so alone. I had amazing new friends out here so that helped me a lot. I kept myself busy and enjoying my life but I missed my son being home with me. It was hard for me to make peace with him being there so unhappy. I guess if he was happy, then things would have been easier for me. This was not meant to be. So, they both decided they were leaving Connecticut together and would be coming home to start their journey together. I was so happy. I could not wait to see them both once they got off the airplane. They both worked and got settled in. New car, new life, new journey to places yet to be.

I loved exploring places and hanging out with my friends. My list of ventures continues to grow as this beautiful state offers so much. I truly feel like I am "HOME", home in my heart and soul, home to where I've always belonged. I never felt this way in Connecticut or any other place that I have traveled to. I find that I spend a lot of time in the Hollywood hills. It just calls to me. I feel euphoria encompass all of me when I am there. It's been 3 and a half years since I arrived here now and I still feel this way. Before moving I felt I had a soul mate connection to someone that I had yet to meet. I felt this way for years. I just knew he was here in California. I also knew that I had quite a soulful journey to embark upon before our paths would connect us to one another. I feel that time is coming soon. There is something special arriving for me this summer, August/September timeframe. And yes, I know, it sure has been a long time in getting here but

I know it could never have happened before this time, and for too many reasons to even begin to write about. So, I'll leave that for another story to be shared once the connection has been made.

I've made amazing new friends this past year. Very beautifully gifted and talented souls, many of them have gifts such as I do so we share a common bond, a connection of divine love and light. Each has told me that I have been here before in another time. I have always known this. I questioned if I was coming back to relive something left undone but everyone has stated the same exact thing. I am here to live my life the very best way that is meant for me to live it. To have a new journey very different from any other past lives. I am here because my heart and soul and my connection to heaven and the angels is much stronger here. It's this way because I am home now. Home in every sense of the word. I belong here. My spirit grows and shines here without the worry of not fitting in as everyone here beats to their own drum here. There is abundance for everyone here and everywhere else too of course. This is my final destination. A place in which to call my own for the rest of my life. Everything has blossomed for me here. I am in love with this beautiful *City of Angels*. I am free. I have my holistic practice currently in Westlake Village but something tells me that someday soon I will be in the Hollywood hills shining my light for all to see and feel. We shall see what's about to unfold. I am excited about the possibilities that lie ahead for me.

Just after the New Year arrived, my glorious new year of 2017, the year in which I have always known that my life was about to be change in ways I have always dreamt of, I felt my father near me and I knew it was time for him to go home to heaven. When we spoke last, around the holidays I told him that it made me sad to know that he was living the way he was with an illness that just took over his body not allowing him to get out on his own anymore. To be trapped inside a failing body for years is no life. We talked about that and I told him he should talk to the angels and tell them when he was ready so they could bring him home. It was a conversation that I knew would be our last. And it was. He died just after the New Year began. I was only able to talk to him through the phone as his wife held the receiver to his ear. He was in a coma and could not respond but I knew he was already out of his body and could hear every word that I said to him. I told him how much I loved him and that Steven and Grammy Lois (his mother), would be there for him. He passed shortly after arriving to the hospital so I booked my flight and flew back to Connecticut for the first time since I had left in 2013. I dreaded it. I truly never wanted to go back to the place that I never felt at home. It was awful. My heart was so sad as much as I was so happy that my dad was no longer sick and suffering so. It was a winter nightmare so the flights were a mess. I tried to just read and focus on the future so I would not have to feel all the miserable people around me continuously complaining about all the canceled flights.

My brother picked me up and I stayed with him and his wife for those few days that felt like an eternity. I love my family but I just wanted to go home. As my dad was cremated and the blizzard was upon us, the service was short and the reception to follow was even shorter as many were not able to make it due to the storm. I broke down in the middle of my eulogy as much as I tried to keep it together. No matter what the circumstances are, it's still not easy to say good-bye to a father, especially when they are still so young. There was just not enough time to be with him when he was alive as he did not make himself available to his children. This made me sad but I understood that he was living his life the best way he knew how to. I loved my dad, just as he was. It's just the way I am. I was happy to see my sisters too and to spend a little time with them. I even got to see Kevin. That made me happy inside. To be able to say hello and hug him once again. It reminded me of the strength he had when I was suffering after losing Steven in 2003. He had a way of always making me feel safe and loved. I appreciated that in him. I felt like things were moving full circle. To truly know that I was no longer connected there allowed me to feel completely free and so much happier inside. This was a gift for me and I knew it. My friend Karen came out which was great to hug that little sweetheart once again. She even came out to my hotel the following night as my flight was cancelled due to the storm. We stayed up all night talking and laughing. We even went out to have sushi in our pajamas. It was a great way to end that trip. I felt much lighter and ready to get home and continue along my path.

My dad and his sweetheart of a mother (Grammy Lois)

The night after I arrived home in California, I went to bed and closed my eyes feeling so thankful that I was so sleepy and knew I would finally get some much-needed rest after such an emotional week. My dad came to see me; Steven brought him to see me. He said, "Momma, I brought you a surprise." His voice was so happy that it made me smile. My dad hugged me and kissed my forehead and he said, "I'm so proud of you kid. I always knew you were special, but I had no idea of the gifts you had and that you could do all of this. It's so beautiful here Dee. I gotta go; I'll see you again soon. Love you kid." And that was it, they were gone. There is not a day that goes by in this incredibly beautiful life of mine that I don't remember to say *Thank You* to God and to the Angels for loving me so very much and for working with me so that I can help so many people along the way. I know what I am here for. I know who I am and I also know that my life is a gift that I will always cherish for as long as I live. And when it's my time to go home to heaven, I know that my journey there will be as equally as beautiful as it was here.

While I was brushing my teeth the other day, this sign fell off the wall and hit me on the head. It's not the first time this has happened. It seemed like a fitting way to end my story. This is only the beginning of what's about to unfold so I'll end this story with this message: *Live the life you have imagined.* xo

The "message" that seems to hit me on the head when I need to be reminded most!

Personal note: I finished writing this story on May 10, 2017 and I know it was no coincidence that the *xo* was typed at 4:44pm. The number 444 has a beautiful meaning and means so much to me.

"There are angels - they're everywhere around you!
You are completely loved, supported, and guided by many
Heavenly beings, and you have nothing to fear."
And so, it is!

Printed in the United States
By Bookmasters